Stain REMOVAL

Stain REMOVAL

BARTY PHILLIPS

BCA

LONDON NEW YORK SYDNEY TORONTO

Safe and effective stain removal requires care and consideration for the fabric or surface being treated, and a knowledge of the cause of the stain. While every effort has been made to check the advice given in this book, the author and publishers cannot accept responsibility for any damage that may occur. If you are in any doubt always consult a specialist cleaner.

Contents

	Introduction	vii
1	*General Principles of Stain Removal*	1
2	*A–Z of Stains on Fabrics*	17
3	*Know Your Fabrics*	60
4	*Household Stain Removal*	72
5	*Prevention is Better than Cure*	95
6	*A Guide to Cleaning Agents*	98
7	*Getting the Best from Dry-Cleaners*	110
	Useful Addresses	116
	Index	118

Introduction

Stains can so often ruin a good piece of clothing, or an expensive carpet. Unfortunately, following your instincts and rushing in with bleach or hot water can fix a stain for ever, quite unnecessarily; whereas the right treatment at the right time can cure the problem completely.

Modern chemicals, up-to-date scientific knowledge and protective fabric finishes have made stain removal much easier but there are no magic answers and many substances will stain permanently if they are not dealt with correctly. In some cases, if the substance is not tackled while still fresh complete removal of the stain may be impossible. Certain substances, particularly those which contain acids, can change the chemistry of the fibre they are spilled on and leave a permanent mark. And in some cases the removal techniques or chemicals are so drastic that they would ruin the fabric anyway.

Chapter 1 gives guidance on the general principles – why certain agents are effective, and why (and when) not to use particular products. Stain removal is really a last resort and it is much better to try to prevent things being spilled in the first place. Once the accident has occurred, it is essential to mop, wipe, scrape or spoon things up before they become stains. There is a very fine line between removing a stain completely and damaging a fabric beyond repair. The object of this book is to help you decide on the best course of action and realise when it is best to leave well alone.

Since most proprietary cleaners are rather expensive, wherever possible I have suggested cheaper alternatives which you may already have in the home. Water, for instance, is one of the best cleaners for non-greasy stains and easily available straight from the tap. You may also have other solvents and absorbents in your kitchen cupboard.

However, many specially formulated proprietary products, whether for general stain removal or for specific stains, are highly effective. In Chapter 5 I have listed the types of products available with explanations of how and why each one works.

Chapter 2 on fabric stains and Chapter 4 on general houseold stains are for quick A–Z reference. Many stains are made up of different ingredients (for instance, white coffee will contain colour from the coffee, and grease from the milk or cream) and more than one type of treatment may be necessary to treat one stain. The treatments are listed in the order in which they should be used for any particular stain.

Lastly, certain fabrics and certain stains are best treated by a professional dry-cleaner. Chapter 6 gives advice on how to deal with dry-cleaners and explains your rights (and responsibilities) as the customer.

I hope you will keep this book in a handy place and that it will get you out of many a spot!

1

*G*eneral *P*rinciples
of *S*tain *R*emoval

Instant Action

Act *the moment* something is spilled. Here are some useful tips on what to do straight away in order to keep damage to the minimum:

- Remove excess spillage at once.
- Sprinkle greasy stains with talcum powder to stop them spreading.
- On tablecloths sprinkle salt on spilled wine, fruit or beetroot juice to stop the stains spreading and to absorb as much as possible.
- Scrape or spoon up solid matter, such as butter, sick or faeces, with the back of a knife or a spatula.
- Chewing gum and mud are the only things best left to dry thoroughly before trying to remove them.
- If the article is washable, hold it under cold running water immediately.
- Blot upholstery and non-washable fabrics with a clean terry towel.

QUICK CHECKLIST OF THE BASIC RULES

1 Always deal with stains as soon as possible. Remove any excess matter at once or flush liquids through with cold water.

2 Don't apply any form of heat before tackling the stain.

3 Check what the stain is and what the fabric is and treat accordingly.

4 Don't attempt to remove the last traces of very stubborn stains. You will damage the fabric.

5 If you give up and take the article to a dry-cleaner, be honest about the methods you have already tried.

Carpets

- Blot or absorb spills with salt or a clean terry towel.
- If you happen to have a soda siphon, spilled liquids can be given a quick squirt which helps to dislodge the stain. Then absorb as much of the liquid as possible with tissues.
- Do not pour white wine over spilled red wine. That just gives you two types of stain to deal with instead of one. Begin by sprinkling salt over the wine stain to absorb as much as possible.

Types of Stain and How to Treat Them

Remember that a stain may be made up of several different substances. For instance, gravy will include grease and possibly blood and colouring. In this case you may have to start with cold water to deal with the blood, then treat with detergent for the grease, then a solvent if the detergent is not enough, and finally a bleach if the colouring proves difficult to remove. In any case always treat the fabric gently and don't rush at it in a panic with a nail brush. Patience will remove many a stain that impetuous cleaning will fix for ever.

Biological Stains

These include blood, egg, faeces, urine and vomit and they should always be soaked or flushed through with cold water before anything else. *Never* start with hot or warm water.

Greasy Stains

These include butter, crayon, engine oil, cosmetics, fat, oil, polish and many foods. Greasy stains should respond to liquid detergent, a dry-cleaning solvent or a proprietary stain remover. Pre-wash treatments will usually work if you catch the stain early and in-wash stain remover sachets may be effective.

Non-Greasy Stains

These include water-based paints, various types of ink, mildew and rust, crude oil, tar, flower and grass stains, fruit stains, iodine, cough mixture and scorch marks. Some of these are very difficult to remove.

Try cold water first, then liquid detergent, then an alkali such as borax or bicarbonate of soda. On non-washable fabrics try a solvent or a proprietary stain remover. Then follow the instructions given in Chapter 2 for the particular type of stain.

Pre-wash and in-wash laundry products may work as well.

Unknown Stains

Treat these with respect and don't rush into drastic cleaning methods.

Begin by soaking in detergent solution if the fabric allows it. Use a proprietary pre-wash stain remover or an in-wash stain remover sachet and wash as usual.

Treat obvious grease marks with a grease solvent.

If there's still a mark after laundering you may have to use a mild bleach such as hydrogen peroxide.

Non-washables can be sponged gently with lukewarm water or treated with a dry-cleaning solvent.

Dried and Set Stains

If a stain has dried or set, start with a mild method of removal. Soaking can be very effective. Repeat if necessary, then progress to something stronger.

Be patient, but remember that a stain which has been left too long or washed in hot water may be impossible to remove.

If the article is fragile or valuable, take it to a dry-cleaner and get expert advice. Keep a note of what you have already used so you can inform the cleaner.

🐛 Removal Techniques

There are several techniques for removing stains. Some can be used one after the other, some are suitable for particular types of stain and some are suitable for particular types of fabric. Here is a brief summary of the major techniques.

Absorbing

This is used to draw out liquids spilled on fabrics and to remove greasy particles from fur and other non-washable fabrics. There are various absorbents, the most common ones being salt, clean white cotton fabric and tissues.

Cold Water Treatment

Pure cold water is one of the best stain removal agents.

Hold washable fabrics under the cold tap or soak them for a few hours in cold water.

Dab non-washable fabrics very gently with cotton wool or tissue squeezed out in cold water. Don't rub, twist or wring; just press gently.

Don't use water at all on dyed wild silk or moiré or any fabric which might show a water mark.

Combined Detergent and Water Treatment

Rub greasy stains with neat washing-up liquid. Use a very soft toothbrush if you want to get the detergent into the

WORKING FROM THE WRONG SIDE

- Many stains, particularly if you catch them quickly, are worse on the face of the fabric, so it is best to draw them out, rather than drive them all the way through. This gives a better chance of removing the stain completely.

- A squirty bottle with a fine-spray nozzle filled with water, or detergent and water, will help to force the stain back the way it came.

- Make sure there's plenty of absorbent padding under the article to soak up the cleaning agent and the stain substance.

- If you can't get at the wrong side of the fabric, absorb as much as you can and then sponge it over and over again, absorbing as much as possible between spongings so as not to get the fabric too wet.

fibres. Then soak or rinse, and finally launder if the fabric is washable. Alternatively, you could soak the item in a mild detergent solution.

Biological Powder Treatment

Biological washing powders may help with protein stains. They are particularly effective when dealing with blood, egg, milk, gravy and perspiration. Always follow the instructions on the packet and make sure the water is lukewarm, not hot.

Don't use on wool or silk or on non-colourfast, flame-resistant or rubberised fabrics.

When soaking colour-fast articles, make sure the whole article is immersed in case the detergent causes a slight overall colour change.

Dry-Cleaning Solvent Treatment

There are a number of solvents, such as methylated spirits and white spirit, which will dissolve grease. There are also several good proprietary stain removers on the market, most of which contain similar solvents or those used by professional dry-cleaners.

If using methylated spirits or white spirit or another 'neat' solvent, use the dab and blot technique (see page 12).

If using a proprietary product, follow the manufacturer's instructions.

TECHNIQUE FOR USING SOLVENTS

1 Place a clean tissue over the stain to absorb moisture, solvent and stain.

2 Working from the back, soak a clean cloth in the solvent and dab the stain, moving in a circular motion from well outside the edge of the stain towards the centre. You can apply the solvent with a medicine dropper if you want to be very precise.

3 Carry on with clean solvent until the stain has vanished. Then dab on water, if the fabric will allow it, to rinse the article. But do not rub.

4 Launder as usual. Or, if not washable, air the article well.

Bleaching

There are several different types of bleach and it is important to use the right one. Some are stronger than others, some will damage particular fabrics. All should be used with patience and care and according to the manufacturer's instructions. It's better to use a weak solution several times than a strong solution once.

Take care not to splash bleach on your clothing when pouring it out of the bottle. It's worth putting on an overall or an old white shirt in case of accidents.

TESTING FOR COLOUR-FASTNESS

Fabrics should be tested for colour-fastness before you try to remove the stain. Some dyes only remain fixed for a limited number of washes or other treatments so you should test every time you treat a garment, especially if you want to leave it in contact with the stain removal agent for any length of time.

Method:

1 Prepare the solvent, bleach or washing powder solution in the proportion in which you plan to use it.

2 Apply the solution to a piece of the garment which won't be seen, such as an inside hem, inside seam or the inside of a pocket.

3 Press the treated area between two pieces of white cloth or tissue.

4 If any colour has been transferred, the fabric is not colour-fast to that particular product and should be dealt with in some other way or by a professional.

Lubricating

Lubricating agents, such as glycerine, lard and margarine, are useful for a number of substances, including chewing gum and grass stains.

Rub some lubricant into the stain and work it in well with your fingers, then wash out.

CHECKLIST FOR STAIN TREATMENT

1 Check the type of stain.

2 Check the fabric and treat according to the most delicate fibre.

3 Check the appropriate method of stain removal, depending on whether or not the fabric is washable.

4 Check the secondary method for removing residual stains.

5 Test for colour-fastness.

Write the answers to your checklist on a piece of paper. Then follow the instructions given in Chapters 2 and 3 for the particular stain, fabric and so on.

🎯 Working Techniques

Here are some general tips on the main stain removal techniques. An ironing board makes a good work table.

Dealing with Solid Matter

- First, remove as much as possible. Use a small wooden spatula or the back of a blunt round-edged table knife, or – if a great deal has been spilled – scoop it up with a spoon.
- Hold the knife at a low angle to the fabric so that it lifts off whatever has been spilled. Don't press too hard and don't scrape.
- If the matter has hardened, you may have to soften it first with water or a solvent.
- It may help to pat gently with a short-bristled brush. Don't use a brushing action.

Dealing with Liquids

- Flush the stain under the cold tap if it is on a washable fabric. If not, soak it up with tissues or some other absorbent material.
- Dissolve the stain in a suitable fluid which will carry the stain with it when flushed out with water or solvent. Washable garments can be soaked in cold water or a water and detergent solution. Non-washables can be treated immediately with a proprietary stain remover or suitable solvent.
- Lay the fabric face down on an absorbent pad of tissues, or use a pad of cotton wool covered by a white, lint-free cloth (such as an old sheet or piece of muslin or several thicknesses of white towel). This helps to draw out the stain.

- When the stain has had a chance to dissolve, flush with water or solvent from well outside the stained area, moving round and round and working towards the centre. This stops the stain spreading any further.

  A plastic bottle with a fine-spray nozzle, of the kind found in hardware shops or garden centres, is useful for flushing out stains. Some chemists sell tiny bottles with spray nozzles which are also good for this job. A medicine dropper is useful for applying solvent to a particular small area.

- If using solvent, blot up any surplus with a clean dry cloth or sponge and use a hairdryer to dry off any remaining solvent.

- If the stain has been treated with water or a detergent solution, rinse thoroughly and wash the garment as usual.

- If powdery particles remain trapped between the fibres after the rest of the stain has dissolved, apply neat liquid detergent and gently work it into the area with your fingers. The particles will become suspended in the detergent and can then be washed away with water.

- Rinse the article three or four times, otherwise dirt will stick to the remains of the detergent and the whole patch will get dirty sooner than the rest.

- If you can't use water, flush with repeated applications of solvent until clean.

- With combination fabrics, remember to treat as appropriate for the more delicate fabric.

Dab and Blot Technique

The dab and blot technique is used for carpets and upholstery which must not become too wet and for non-washable fabrics.

- Begin by dabbing the stain with a suitable stain removal agent, whether it's water, solvent or bleach. Then blot dry. Dab with stain remover again, and blot dry. Do this as many times as necessary. It is much better to do this 'little and often', rather than use too strong a solution or too rough a treatment just once.

- When dabbing and blotting, just press firmly onto the stain. Don't rub or brush it.
- A surprising amount of moisture can be brought out of a carpet by standing on a towel or tissues with a little pressure. Again, don't rub or scrub.

Cleaning Special Textiles

Never try to wash or dry-clean textiles you think may be of historic importance or which are made of some especially delicate or precious fabric. Consult a professional textile conservator. Your local museum should be able to advise.

🐾 Stain Removal Kit

You may already have many of these items in your home. It's useful to have a drawer or box for your stain removal kit so that you can lay your hands on the necessary items quickly in an emergency. Of course, you don't need to have all these things. This is simply a checklist from which to make your selection of detergents, solvents, lubricants, bleaches and proprietary products.

Do remember to label all substances clearly and keep out of the reach of children. (See also the section on Safety First, page 16.)

Cleaning Substances

Washing-up liquid (detergent)
Travel Wash (detergent)
Stergene (detergent)
Household ammonia (alkali)

THREE IMPORTANT DON'TS

1 Don't apply any heat to the fabric before tackling a stain. Many food stains contain albumen or similar proteins which are 'fixed' by heat. In other words, don't wash it in hot water; always flush with cold water first.

2 Don't try to remove every trace of very stubborn stains. It may be better to leave the last vestiges of the stain showing, rather than risk ruining the article altogether by applying too much bleach or solvent or rubbing too long or too hard.

3 Don't tackle complicated stains on delicate fabrics yourself. Consult a dry-cleaner.

Bicarbonate of soda (alkali)
Borax (alkali)
Washing soda crystals (alkali)
Sodium perborate (alkali)
Acetic acid or white vinegar (acid)
Citric acid or lemon juice (acid)
Methylated spirits (solvent)
Acetone or a non-oily nail varnish remover (solvent)
Amyl acetate (solvent)
Cellulose thinners (solvent)
Turpentine (solvent)
White spirit (solvent)
Liquid lighter fuel (solvent)
Hydrogen peroxide (bleach)
Household or chlorine bleach
Salt (absorbent and alkali)
Bran, talcum powder, French chalk, fuller's earth
  (absorbents)
Eucalyptus oil
Glycerine (lubricant)
Vaseline (lubricant)
Margarine (lubricant)
Lard (lubricant)
Your choice of proprietary stain removers
Proprietary pre-wash treatment
Proprietary in-wash treatment
Upholstery stain remover
Carpet stain remover

Tools and Equipment

A box or roll of paper tissues
A small sponge
White cotton wool
White terry towelling or old cotton sheeting
Medicine dropper for powerful solvents
Squirty bottle with fine-spray nozzle

Stain Removal

Fine sandpaper for cleaning suede
Suede brush
Soft old toothbrush or nail brush
Clothes brush

Safety First

Many stain removers, including proprietary ones, are caustic, poisonous and/or give off toxic fumes. Treat all such substances with caution and always follow the manufacturer's instructions. (See Chapter 5 for details of specific cleaning agents.)

- Keep all stain removal substances out of the reach of children and pets, preferably in a locked cupboard.
- Always label everything clearly.
- Buy and store all cleaning substances in small quantities.
- Do not decant solvents into other containers.
- Do not pour used solvents back into the bottle.
- Use rubber gloves when working with cleaning agents.
- Never smoke while working with stain removal agents.
- Work in a well-ventilated room, preferably with the window open.

Particular Hazards to Guard Against:

- Methylated spirits are highly flammable and poisonous.
- Spirits of salts, amyl acetate, liquid lighter fuel, turpentine, white spirit, cellulose thinners and non-oily nail varnish remover are all flammable, dangerous to inhale and poisonous if swallowed.
- Ammonia gives off unpleasant fumes and should not come into contact with eyes, skin or clothing. It is also poisonous.
- Never mix one type of cleaner with another unless specified.

2

A–Z of
Stains on Fabrics

The instructions in this chapter will work better if you have already read the basic information in Chapter 1 and gained a general understanding of the processes involved.

The advice is given in the sequence in which it should be used, starting with initial fast-reaction treatment. In each case, we begin with instructions for washable items, then non-washable fabrics, and finally upholstery and carpets.

Remember to work from the wrong side if possible and place an absorbent pad under the right side to absorb both the cleaning agent and the staining substance. Detailed instructions on using particular cleaning agents are given in Chapter 5.

Acids (Sulphuric/hydrochloric/acetic/vinegar)

- Immediately plunge into cold water.
- Dab on household ammonia solution (see page 50) or 1 teaspoon bicarbonate of soda dissolved in ¼ pint (150 ml) cold water.
- Rinse thoroughly.
- For carpets, dab and mop up repeatedly so as not to saturate the fibres.
- Acids may cause permanent damage.

BASIC STAIN REMOVAL SEQUENCE

1 Emergency treatment: scoop solids; absorb or flush liquids with cold water.

2 Detergent solution: lubricate, wash or soak washable fabrics; dab and blot non-washable fabrics.

3 Solvent treatment: see Technique for Using Solvents, page 8.

4 Bleach: soak or apply direct to stain with a medicine dropper (see Bleaching, page 8).

Adhesives

Lift off as much deposit as possible and then treat according to type of adhesive.

Contact Adhesive

- Dab lightly on the wrong side with non-oily nail varnish remover (*not* on acetate or triacetate fabrics). Or dab with amyl acetate on a sponge or cotton wool.
- On acetate and triacetate fabrics use amyl acetate, but test for colour-fastness first (see page 9).

Cyanoacrylates ('superglues')

- These are soluble in water.
- Soak in cold water and wash as usual.
- For non-washable fabrics and carpets, dab and blot repeatedly with cold water.

Epoxy Resin (e.g. Araldite)

- Stains which have dried are impossible to remove.
- Dab fresh adhesive on the wrong side with cellulose thinners.
- On synthetic fibres use lighter fuel.
- On synthetic pile carpet use lighter fuel. Dried stains can be trimmed off with a pair of sharp scissors. Be careful to snip off only the minimum.

Latex Adhesive

- Remove with a damp cloth while still wet.
- If already dried, scrape off deposit (if this is possible without damaging the fabric) and dab the residual stain with a solvent or paint brush cleaner or an eraser.

- Do not try paint strippers such as Nitromors or Poly-strippa which contain chemicals damaging to fibres.

Model-Making Cement

- This is impossible to remove once it has dried.
- Wipe off as much as possible without spreading the adhesive.
- Dab what's left with a solvent.

PVA

- Remove with methylated spirits.

Alkalis (washing soda/caustic soda)

- Wash immediately in warm water, otherwise the fabric may be permanently damaged.
- Rinse in white vinegar solution (see page 50). Final rinse in water.
- For non-washable fabrics and carpets, dab and blot repeatedly with warm water, then cold water and white vinegar, as above.

Antiperspirants

- Treat with a solvent.
- Follow with household ammonia solution (see page 50) if necessary. Rinse.
- Launder as usual, putting a laundry stain removal sachet in the wash.

🐾 Ballpoint Pen

- Most ballpoint pen inks are completely soluble in methylated spirits. Dab or flush repeatedly, using a medicine dropper if you have one, so as not to waste the meths.
- Air or rinse thoroughly.
- For suede, rub gently with abrasive paper.

🐾 Beers

- Flush or sponge with water.
- Flush or dab with neat white vinegar and, if necessary, soak in biological detergent. (Don't use biological detergent on wool or silk.)
- Treat with hydrogen peroxide solution (see page 50) and rinse in cold water.
- Wash at high temperature if the fabric allows it.
- For carpets, dab and blot repeatedly. Don't saturate. Use a proprietary carpet stain remover.

🐾 Beetroot

- Sponge as quickly as possible with cold water. Or soak in cold water overnight.
- Work neat liquid detergent into the stain and rinse.
- Stretch the dampened stain over a bowl, sprinkle borax onto it and pour boiling water over.
- For wool, do not rub the stain. Just let the water run through the fabric, or squeeze it gently in the detergent solution.

🐾 Bird Droppings

- Lift off excess with a spatula or the back of a knife.

Stain Removal

- Soak washable articles in warm biological detergent solution.
- Treat non-washable fabrics with household ammonia solution (see page 50), then with white vinegar. Rinse with cold water. Or dab and blot. If the droppings are stained with berries, bleach carefully with hydrogen peroxide solution (see page 50).

🐾 Blackberry

See FRUIT AND FRUIT JUICES.

🐾 Blackcurrant

See FRUIT AND FRUIT JUICES.

🐾 Blood

- Hold under the cold tap or soak in cold salt water at once. *Do not* use warm water.
- Wash or clean according to fabric.
- If the stain has hardened, soak in biological detergent solution or hydrogen peroxide solution (see page 50).
- For non-washable fabrics, dab the stain with cold water or use a proprietary stain remover.
- For carpets and upholstery, flush out fresh stains with a squirt from a soda siphon if you have one, or dab and blot with cold water. Then treat with a proprietary carpet stain remover.

Brandy

See SPIRITS.

 Butter

- Lift off as much as possible with a spatula or the back of a knife.
- Wash at high temperature if possible.
- Treat non-washable fabrics with a solvent and dry with a hair dryer or treat with a proprietary stain remover.
- For carpets, use a proprietary carpet stain remover.

 Candle Wax

- Allow to cool and harden (freeze for an hour or so if you can), then crack off the hardened pieces. If the fabric is loosely woven, don't try to pull the wax off. Go straight to the next stage.
- Sandwich the fabric between sheets of blotting paper or tissues and press with a warm iron on the lowest setting. Keep replacing the paper as it becomes saturated.
- Apply a stain remover to any last traces of wax.
- Launder, if possible, to remove any residual colour.
- Bleach if necessary.
- For carpets and upholstery, after removing the bulk of the wax, place blotting paper or tissues over the mark and iron gently on the lowest setting. Don't allow the iron to touch the pile; remove any residual stains with methylated spirits.

 Car Polish and Wax

- Dab with a solvent or a proprietary stain remover.

- Soak in detergent solution.
- Launder if possible.
- For non-washable fabrics, just use several applications of the solvent, absorbing each before applying the next.

Caramel

- Rinse with cold water.
- Rub in neat liquid detergent and rinse.
- Treat with hydrogen peroxide solution (see page 50).
- For non-washable fabrics, use a proprietary stain remover.
- Treat carpets with cleaning agents as above, using the dab and blot technique (see page 12). Or use a carpet stain remover.

Carbon Paper

- Use neat liquid detergent and rinse well with cold water.
- If the stains remain, treat with a few drops of household ammonia and then again with detergent. Repeat several times if necessary.
- Dab non-washable fabrics with methylated spirits.
- For acetate fabrics, use a proprietary stain remover.

Chewing Gum

- Freeze for an hour or so until it becomes hard. Then break off the bits.
- Holding a bag of ice cubes over the gum will harden it quickly, or Holloway's Chewing Gum Remover will do the job by means of a spray (see address on page 117).
- Treat any residual mark with methylated spirits or white spirit.

- Proprietary hand cleaners, available from hardware shops, can be rubbed in until the gum dissolves.
- Other proprietary chewing gum removers are available from hardware stores and supermarkets.
- Launder if possible.
- For upholstery, after cracking off the bits as above, brush or pick any deposits off by hand. They could be disastrous in the vacuum cleaner.
- If the chewing gum is stuck in someone's hair, use the freezing method or lubricate the gum with margarine or glycerine and slide it off. Then shampoo the hair.

Chocolate/Cocoa

- Lift off excess with the back of a knife and rinse in cold water.
- Soak in biological detergent solution.
- Launder as usual, putting a laundry stain removal sachet in with the wash.
- If the stain persists, wet the mark and sprinkle with borax powder, stretch the fabric over a bowl and pour hot water over it. Rinse.
- For non-washable fabrics, scrape off as above. Use a proprietary stain remover.
- Dried stains should be sponged well with a borax solution (see page 50) using the dab and blot technique (see page 12). Or use an upholstery spotting kit. Treat any remaining stain with solvent or proprietary stain remover.
- For carpets, first remove the deposit with the back of a knife. Then treat the stained area with carpet stain remover. Repeat if necessary. If any stain remains, rub in equal parts of glycerine and warm water. Leave for 1–2 hours, then dab with clean water and blot repeatedly. Repeat the glycerine treatment if necessary.

Stain Removal

Chutney

See JAM.

Coca Cola and Pepsi Cola

- Rinse in cold water or soak in detergent and water.
- Treat with a dessertspoon of methylated spirits plus a few drops of white vinegar. Rinse.
- Launder as usual.
- For carpets and upholstery, use the same cleaning agents and the dab and blot technique (see page 12).

Cod Liver Oil

Fresh stains are easily removed; whereas old stains are practically impossible to get rid of, even with bleach.
- Absorb as much as possible with a white cotton cloth or tissues.
- Apply a solvent from the back of the stain.
- Sponge baby clothes with a strong solution of washing-up liquid and wash as usual, putting a laundry stain removal sachet in with the wash.
- Sponge woollens immediately with mild detergent solution – don't rub. Then wash as usual.
- For non-washable fabrics, use a proprietary stain remover.
- For heavy stains, repeat the cleaning process after a few days.
- If the stains have dried, use methylated spirits or a proprietary stain remover.
- For carpets, use a carpet stain remover.

🐾 Coffee

- Soak in biological detergent solution.
- Launder as usual, putting a laundry stain removal sachet in with the wash.
- For non-washable fabrics, lubricate old stains with glycerine solution (equal parts glycerine and warm water). Leave for 1 hour, then rinse well and blot well.
- For carpets, flush out stain with a squirt from a soda siphon if you have one, or sponge and blot with water. Treat with carpet stain remover if necessary.
- If the stain is milky coffee, use a carpet stain remover. When dry, remove traces with a solvent. Or use a specially formulated stain remover.
- Dried stains may come out with repeated soda siphon squirts but make sure the carpet dries out between squirts.

🐾 Cough Mixture

See MEDICINES.

🐾 Crayon

- Dab the marks with a solvent or a proprietary stain remover.
- Flush out any residual colour with methylated spirits. Don't take measures that are any more drastic than this or you may remove the original colour too.

🐾 Cream

- Remove any excess with a spoon or the back of a knife.
- Rinse in cold water or soak in biological detergent solution and rinse.

- Launder as usual, putting a laundry stain removal sachet in with the wash.
- For non-washable fabrics, scrape off excess. Use a little solvent and then dab carefully. Don't rub. Or you could use a proprietary stain remover.
- For carpets, blot or scrape up excess. Use a little methylated spirits or white spirit and then a carpet stain remover.

🐾 Crude Oil (found on beaches)

- Soften with white spirit, Vaseline, lard or glycerine and then gently scrape away as much as you can.
- Flush with a solvent or use a proprietary stain remover.

🐾 Curry

- Remove the deposit with a spoon or the back of a knife.
- Soften with glycerine solution (equal parts glycerine and warm water).
- Soak in biological detergent or household ammonia solution (see page 50).
- Launder, putting a laundry stain removal sachet in with the wash.
- Bleach if necessary.
- For non-washable fabrics, remove deposit. Then apply household ammonia or borax solution (see page 50), using the dab and blot technique (see page 12).
- If necessary get the garment professionally dry-cleaned *before* you do too much damage.

🐾 Dyes

- Soak colour-fast fabrics in a biological detergent solu-

tion, but not wool, silk, rubberised or flame-retardant fabrics.
- Launder, putting a colour removal product, such as Colour Run or Dygon, in with the wash.
- Sponge silk and wool with hydrogen peroxide solution (see page 50) or soak for 15 minutes in the same solution.
- For carpets, upholstery and non-washable fabrics, dab with a sponge soaked in methylated spirits (*not* on acetate or triacetate), to which a few drops of household ammonia have been added.
- If in doubt, get the garment professionally dry-cleaned.

🐾 Egg

- Rinse in cold water.
- Soak in biological detergent solution, then rinse in cold water.
- When dry, treat with solvent if necessary.
- Launder as usual.
- For whites, soak stubborn stains in 1 pint hydrogen peroxide solution (see page 50), with 5 drops household ammonia added.

🐾 Embroidery Transfers

See TRANSFER PATTERNS.

🐾 Engine Oil

This is often very difficult to remove.
- Rub in neat liquid detergent and rinse in cold water.
- Then flush with a solvent or proprietary stain remover. Repeat several times.

- For carpets, use the same cleaning agents but follow the dab and blot technique (see page 12). Then use a carpet stain remover.

Eye Make-up

Eyebrow Pencil

- Dab on solvent.
- Dab with a few drops of household ammonia. Rinse in cold water.

Eye Shadow

- Wet the fabric, then rub in neat liquid detergent and rinse in cold water.
- Let the fabric dry and treat with methylated spirits. Repeat if necessary.

Fat, Cold

See BUTTER.

- Dripping which has bits of gravy in it should be scraped off. Then the item should be soaked, sponged or sprayed with cold water or a biological detergent solution. Treat any remaining stain with solvent or proprietary stain remover.

Fat, Hot

- Remove as much as possible with the back of a knife.
- Treat with neat liquid detergent and rinse in cold water.
- Repeat if necessary.
- Launder as usual, putting a laundry stain removal sachet in with the wash.

- Treat non-washable fabrics with a solvent or proprietary stain remover.

🟣 Felt-Tip Pen

- Lubricate the stain with soap or glycerine.
- Launder as usual.
- Write to the manufacturer for advice if necessary.
- Sponge non-washable fabrics with methylated spirits.

🟣 Foundation Cream

- Wet the fabric and treat with neat liquid detergent. Rinse in cold water.
- Use talcum powder or some other absorbent to draw out the stain. Leave for 2 hours, then brush out gently, using a watercolour or make-up brush for fine fabrics.
- For very greasy foundation creams, use a solvent or proprietary stain remover.

🟣 French Polish (Shellac)

- Act immediately. Dab the stain with methylated spirits (*not* on acetate or triacetate fabrics).
- Repeat until all traces of the stain have vanished.
- If the stain has dried, it may be possible to soften it enough with methylated spirits to launder or sponge it out.

🟣 Fruit and Fruit Juices

- Rinse or flush with cold water.
- Treat with neat mild detergent. Rinse in cold water.

- If necessary, treat with household ammonia or hydrogen peroxide solution (see page 50).
- Wash at high temperature if fabric allows it; or with biological detergent at low temperature, putting a laundry stain removal sachet in with the wash.
- Sponge non-washable fabrics with cold water and blot dry. Or use a proprietary stain remover.
- For silk, nylon and wool, use a proprietary colour remover, such as Colour Run or Dygon, and a proprietary stain remover.
- For table linen, hold the stained part over a basin and pour hot water through. Lubricate any residual stain with glycerine solution (equal parts glycerine and warm water), leave for 1 hour and launder as usual.
- For carpets, absorb as much as possible with paper towels immediately. Shampoo the area. When dry, dab with a cloth moistened in methylated spirits.
- Loosen dried stains with glycerine solution.

Furniture Polish

- Remove excess polish with a spatula or the back of a knife.
- Treat with a solvent or a proprietary stain remover.
- Launder if possible, putting a laundry stain removal sachet in with the wash.

Gin

See SPIRITS.

Glue

See ADHESIVES.

🌸 Grass

- Lubricate with glycerine. For heavier marks, dab with methylated spirits.
- Launder as usual, putting a laundry stain removal sachet in with the wash.
- For non-washable fabrics, use a proprietary stain remover. There are some specially formulated for grass stains, such as DeSolvIt2 or the appropriate Stain Devil.

🌸 Gravy

- Lift off any deposit with a spatula or the back of a knife.
- Sponge or soak with cold water.
- Use a solvent or a proprietary stain remover.
- Launder as usual, putting a laundry stain removal sachet in with the wash.
- Soak dried stains in biological detergent solution. Then try a specially formulated proprietary stain remover, such as K2r Stain Devils Sauce and Spice Remover.
- For non-washable fabrics, remove deposit. Then sponge with cold water. Or you could apply absorbent powder or use a solvent or proprietary stain remover.

🌸 Grease

- Remove deposit with the back of a knife.
- Wash at high temperature if fabric allows it, using washing soda or borax to emulsify the grease and release the dirt.
- Try dissolving the grease in hydrogen peroxide solution (see page 50) with a little paraffin oil added.
- Use a solvent for residual stains. Dry with a hair dryer.
- Launder if the fabric allows it.
- For wool and silk, absorb the grease with fuller's earth or

French chalk mixed to a paste with water. Put onto the stain and brush out gently when dry.

- Some grease marks on wool and silk can be removed by sandwiching the fabric between tissues and pressing with a cool iron.

Hair Dye

- Treat with neat liquid detergent.
- Wash as usual.
- Repeat if necessary.
- Most old dye stains will not respond if they have been left too long.
- For non-washable fabrics, use a proprietary stain remover.

Henna

- Rinse with cold water. Treat with neat liquid detergent. Rinse. Treat again if necessary.
- Follow with methylated spirits (*not* on acetate or triacetate fabrics), or amyl acetate, then hydrogen peroxide solution (see page 50). Rinse.

Hair Lacquer

- Treat with amyl acetate.
- Flush with a solvent.

Hair Oil

See FAT or GREASE.

Hand Cream

- Remove excess with the back of a knife.

- Wet the fabric, then rub in neat liquid detergent. Rinse in cold water.
- If necessary, treat with a solvent.
- Treat non-washable fabrics with a proprietary stain remover such as Dabitoff.

Honey

- Spoon off excess.
- Rinse with cold water.
- Rub in neat liquid detergent. Rinse.
- If necessary, treat with hydrogen peroxide solution (see page 50). Rinse.
- Treat non-washable fabrics with a proprietary stain remover.

Ice Cream

- Remove deposit with a spoon or the back of a knife.
- Soak in warm detergent solution.
- If there's still a greasy mark when the fabric has dried, treat with a solvent or proprietary stain remover.
- Launder as usual, putting a laundry stain removal sachet in with the wash.
- For non-washable fabrics, use a proprietary stain remover.
- For carpets and upholstery, use a carpet stain remover or upholstery spotting kit.

Indelible Pencil

Not easy to remove, as the name implies.
- Flush two or three times with methylated spirits or a proprietary stain remover.

- Repeat as necessary.
- Treat residual stain with liquid detergent solution containing a few drops of household ammonia. Rinse with cold water.
- Launder if possible, putting a laundry stain removal sachet in with the wash.
- If the stain persists, treat with hydrogen peroxide solution (see page 50). Rinse.
- If in doubt, take to a professional dry-cleaner.

Ink

Catch while wet if possible, although even then you may not get the stain out completely.
- Flush with cold water immediately and treat with neat liquid detergent from the back of the stain. Rinse in cold water.
- Repeat until no more colour comes out.
- Treat residual stain with lemon juice, rinse in household ammonia solution (see page 50). Then rinse again. Or try Stain Devils Mould and Ink Remover.
- Dried ink needs drastic treatment. Use Stain Devils Rust and Iron Mould Remover. Or you could use a household bleach solution (see page 50). Test the fabric first.
- The Parker Pen Company will give advice on inks used in any of their pens (see page 117).

Ballpoint Pen Ink

See BALLPOINT PEN.

Coloured Writing Ink

- Treat with neat liquid detergent, then rinse with cold water.

- Repeat several times.
- If necessary, treat with hydrogen peroxide solution (see page 50). Rinse.
- Treat with Stain Devils Mould and Ink Remover.
- If in doubt, take to a professional dry-cleaner.

Duplicating Ink

- Flush with white spirit.
- Treat residual stain with neat liquid detergent. Rinse in cold water.
- Repeat several times.
- If in doubt, take to a professional dry-cleaner.

Duplicating Powder and Printing Toner

- Keep dry at all costs. It should then brush out or vacuum completely. Using any sort of solvent will really make a mess.

Felt-Tip Ink

See FELT-TIP PEN.

Indelible Pencil/Indian Ink

See INDELIBLE PENCIL.

Marking Ink

- Treat with a solvent.
- Repeat several times.
- If in doubt, take to a professional dry-cleaner.

Printer Toner

See DUPLICATING POWDER.

Printing Ink

- Flush with methylated spirits.
- Treat residual stain with neat washing-up liquid. Rinse in cold water.
- Repeat as necessary.
- If in doubt, take to a professional dry-cleaner.

Typewriter Ribbon

- Flush two or three times with a multi-purpose solvent, then methylated spirits.
- Treat with liquid detergent solution containing a few drops of ammonia.
- If necessary, follow with hydrogen peroxide solution (see page 50). Rinse with cold water.

Iodine

- Moisten with water and place in the sun.
- Dab with methylated spirits.
- Place a cotton wool bud soaked in methylated spirits on the stain. Leave it, keeping it soaked with meths for several hours.
- Or you could try one of the proprietary products formulated to deal with iodine stains such as De SolvIt 2 or Stain Devils Coffee and Tea Remover.

Iron Mould

- Cover the stain with salt. Squeeze lemon juice over the salt. Leave for an hour. Rinse well with cold water.
- Repeat several times.
- For white fabrics, use a proprietary rust remover such as Holloway's (see page 117).

- If in doubt about non-washable fabrics, take to a professional dry-cleaner.

🦋 Jam

- Remove deposit with a spatula or spoon or the back of a knife. Don't scrape too hard.
- Rinse with cold water or liquid detergent solution. Rinse.
- If necessary, treat with hydrogen peroxide solution (see page 50). Rinse.
- For non-washable fabrics, use a proprietary stain remover.

🦋 Ketchup

- Remove deposit with a spatula or spoon or the back of a knife. Don't scrape too hard.
- Rinse with cold water or liquid detergent solution. Rinse.
- Soak in biological detergent solution.
- For non-washable fabrics, use a solvent or proprietary stain remover.

🦋 Lead Pencil

- Rub gently with a pencil eraser.
- Treat with methylated spirits, white spirit or proprietary stain remover.

🦋 Lipstick

- Remove excess carefully with the back of a knife.

- Treat with methylated spirits or some other solvent or a proprietary stain remover.
- Repeat two or three times. Rinse with cold water.
- Treat with liquid detergent solution. Rinse.
- If necessary, treat with household ammonia solution (see page 50). Rinse.
- For non-washable fabrics, dab gently with eucalyptus oil or use a proprietary stain remover.
- Indelible lipstick can be softened with glycerine solution (using equal parts glycerine and water).
- Residual stains should be bleached out with hydrogen peroxide solution (see page 50).

 Liqueurs

- Rinse with cold water.
- Launder as usual.
- For non-washable fabrics and upholstery, use a proprietary stain remover or upholstery spotting kit.
- For carpets, use a carpet stain remover.

Lotions

See GREASE.

Margarine

See CREAM.

Marmalade

See JAM.

40

🐾 Mascara

- Treat with neat liquid detergent.
- Treat with household ammonia solution (see page 50).
- If necessary, follow with a solvent or proprietary stain remover.

🐾 Mayonnaise

- Remove deposit with a spoon or the back of a knife.
- Sponge with cold water (not hot). Use a biological detergent to soak if possible, then launder as usual.
- For non-washable fabrics treat dry fabric with a proprietary stain remover such as Dabitoff or K2r or Stain Devils Sauce and Spice Remover.

🐾 Meat Juices

- Rinse with cold water.
- Treat with biological detergent in warm, not hot water. Rinse.
- Allow to dry before treating with a solvent or proprietary stain remover.

🐾 Medicines

- Sponge with warm water.
- Launder as usual.
- Apply methylated spirits for any residual stain.

🐾 Metal Polish

- Absorb as much as possible with tissues or cotton cloth.

- Saturate with cold water.
- Apply a solvent or proprietary stain remover.
- For non-washable fabrics, absorb as much as possible. Allow to dry. Brush well. Treat remaining marks with a solvent or proprietary stain remover.

Mildew

Regular washing will reduce marks, but once they do appear:
- Flush through from the wrong side with household bleach solution (see page 50).
- Laundering usually removes fresh mildew.
- For white cottons, treat any residual stain with hydrogen peroxide solution (see page 50). Or use household bleach solution (except on cottons and linens with special finishes).
- For coloured fabrics, dampen the stained areas, rub with hard soap or Vanish and dry in the sun.
- Non-washable fabrics and upholstery should be sprayed with a proprietary fungicide, such as Fungo (see page 117). The smell may take several days to disappear.
- For plastic shower curtains, sponge on a weak solution of household bleach or antiseptic. For heavy marking, swab with mild detergent solution, and rinse with a proprietary fungicide (see page 117).
- Leather should be wiped over with undiluted antiseptic mouthwash. Wipe dry with a soft cloth, then polish.

Milk

Rinse with cold water.
- Treat with neat liquid biological detergent. Rinse.
- For non-washable fabrics, try a solvent or a proprietary product.

🐾 Mineral Oil

- Dab with a solvent or a proprietary stain remover.
- Saturate fabric with cold water, then squeeze lemon juice over while wet. Rinse with cold water.
- Launder as usual, putting a laundry stain removal sachet in with the wash.
- For non-washable fabrics, don't use water. Repeat the solvent treatment.

🐾 Modelling Dough

- Carefully scrape or pick off as much as possible.
- Dab with a solvent to dissolve deposit.
- Launder as usual.

🐾 Mud

- Allow to dry completely.
- Brush off the dried mud.
- Launder if appropriate, putting a laundry stain removal sachet in with the wash.
- Any remaining stains can be treated with a solvent, then methylated spirits, then neat liquid detergent. Rinse in cold water.
- Allow non-washable fabrics to dry, then lightly brush mud off. Sponge remaining marks with warm detergent solution. Wipe with a cloth wrung out in clean water. Blot well.
- Or you could try one of the proprietary cleaners specially formulated for dealing with mud.

Mustard

- Rinse with cold water.
- Treat with detergent solution.
- Launder as usual, putting a laundry stain removal sachet in with the wash.
- Treat non-washable fabrics with a proprietary stain remover.

Mystery Stains

See UNIDENTIFIED STAINS.

Nail Varnish

- Absorb as much as possible with tissues.
- Treat with acetone (*not* on acetate or triacetate fabrics) or amyl acetate. Don't use oily nail varnish remover.
- Flush out with white spirit.

Nicotine

See TOBACCO.

Oil

See MINERAL OIL, VEGETABLE OIL.

Ointment

- Remove deposit with the back of a knife.
- Treat with a solvent.

- Treat with liquid detergent solution. Rinse with cold water.
- For old stains, soak overnight; then launder, putting a laundry stain removal sachet in with the wash.
- Treat non-washable fabrics with a solvent as above, but not liquid detergent. Or use an absorbent, such as fuller's earth or French chalk, to draw out the stain.

Paint

Act while the paint is still wet. Dry paint is almost impossible to remove.

Acrylic Paint

- Blot with tissues.
- Wash out with detergent solution.
- Use proprietary stain remover or methylated spirits.
- Launder if possible.

Emulsion and Water-Based Paints

- Lift or spoon off as much as possible.
- Use methylated spirits to remove residual colour (*not* on acetate or triacetate fabrics).
- Or use a proprietary paint brush cleaner or a specially formulated proprietary stain remover.
- Launder as usual.
- Treat non-washable fabrics as above but sponge instead of laundering.
- Delicate fabrics should be taken to a professional dry-cleaner.
- Large areas of dried emulsion on upholstery, carpets or clothes should be referred to a professional dry-cleaner.

Enamel Paint

Treat with methylated spirits or a proprietary paint remover while still wet.

Oil-Based Paints (Gloss Paint and Undercoat)

- Dab wet paint carefully with white spirit or paint brush cleaner and sponge with cold water.
- Repeat if necessary.
- Launder as usual.
- For carpets and upholstery, use a carpet stain remover or upholstery spotting kit. Or use a chemical paint remover but test the fabric first because this is a drastic remedy.
- Bad marks and spills on acetate and viscose fabrics should be taken to a professional dry-cleaner.

Watercolour Paint

- Rinse in cold water.
- Wet fabric and treat with household ammonia solution (see page 50). Rinse well.
- Or wet the fabric and treat with equal parts of hydrogen peroxide and water.

🌣 Perfume

- Rinse immediately.
- If the stain has dried, lubricate with glycerine solution (equal parts of glycerine and warm water).
- Leave for an hour or so before laundering as usual.
- Dab non-washable fabrics with a cloth wrung out in warm water. Don't get the fabric too wet. Blot dry. Repeat as necessary.
- Take expensive clothes to a professional dry-cleaner.

👕 Perspiration

- Wet the fabric and treat with a weak household ammonia solution (see page 50).
- Or soak in biological detergent (but not wool or silk).
- Launder as usual.
- Persistent stains can be dampened, treated with hydrogen peroxide solution (see page 50) and laundered again.
- If anti-perspirant deodorant is combined with the stain, treat with a solvent, then household ammonia solution, as above.
- If a dye is combined with the stain, white vinegar can sometimes remove it. Or launder, adding a proprietary colour such as Colour Run or Dygon, to the wash.
- White linen and cotton can be saturated with 1 eggcup methylated spirits to which 5 drops of household ammonia have been added.
- For silk and wool, use hydrogen peroxide solution (see page 50). Soak for 5–15 minutes, and rinse thoroughly. Wash or dry-clean as usual.
- For viscose, nylon and polyester, use household bleach solution (see page 50) but don't soak for longer than 15 minutes. Rinse thoroughly in cold water.
- Dab non-washable fabrics with a solution of white vinegar and water (see page 50). Follow with methylated spirits if the dye has been affected (but not on acetate or triacetate fabrics).
- Men's suits are often lined with non-washable fabrics and should be cleaned by a professional dry-cleaner.

👕 Plasticine/Play Dough

See MODELLING DOUGH.
- For non-washable fabrics, treat as above, then sponge gently with warm water and blot dry at once.

Stain Removal

❀ Putty

- Gently pick off as much as possible.
- Treat with a solvent.
- Treat any residual stain with neat liquid detergent. Rinse in cold water.
- Launder as usual.
- Or use a specially formulated proprietary stain remover.

❀ Raspberry/Ribena

See FRUIT AND FRUIT JUICES.

❀ Rouge

- Treat two or three times with a solvent or methylated spirits.
- Treat with neat liquid detergent, then household ammonia solution (see page 50). Rinse in warm water.
- Launder as usual.
- Treat non-washable fabrics with a solvent or a proprietary stain remover.

❀ Rum

See SPIRITS.

❀ Rust

See IRON MOULD.

🐾 Salad Dressing

See VEGETABLE OIL.

🐾 Sauces

- Remove any deposit and rinse in cold water.
- Treat with neat liquid detergent for the grease.
- When dry, dab with methylated spirits. Rinse.
- Treat residual stains by soaking in biological detergent solution. Rinse.
- Launder as usual, putting a laundry stain removal sachet in with the wash.
- For non-washable fabrics, remove deposit. Treat with methylated spirits (*not* on acetate or triacetate fabrics) or use a specially formulated proprietary stain remover.

🐾 Scent

See PERFUME.

🐾 Scorch Marks

- Lubricate the scorched area with 1 part glycerine to 2 parts water, rubbing it in with your fingertips.
- Soak in a borax solution (see page 50). Leave for 15 minutes. Then rinse well in warm water.
- Bad scorch marks are impossible to remove because the fibres will have been damaged.
- White fabrics can be carefully bleached in a hydrogen peroxide solution (see page 50).

DILUTING CLEANING AGENTS

These are the normal dilutions of commonly used cleaning agents. If different dilutions are required they will be given under the particular stain.

Household ammonia	1 teaspoon ammonia to 1 pint (600 ml) water
Biological detergent	Follow manufacturer's instructions
Borax	1 tablespoon borax to 1 pint (600 ml) warm water
Glycerine	1 part glycerine to 1 part warm water
Household chlorine bleach: mild solution strong solution	2 teaspoons bleach to ½ pint (300 ml) cool water 1 part bleach to 1 part water
Hydrogen peroxide	1 part 20 vol. peroxide to 6 parts water
Lemon juice	Use neat
Mild liquid detergent	1 squirt in a bowl of water or use neat
Mild disinfectant	1 teaspoon disinfectant to ½ pint (300 ml) warm water
White vinegar	1 tablespoon vinegar to 9 fl oz (250 ml) warm water

Shoe Polish

- Remove deposit carefully with the back of a knife so as not to spread it.
- Treat with a solvent or proprietary stain remover.
- Treat with liquid detergent solution with a few drops of household ammonia added.
- Treat residual stains with methylated spirits. Rinse with warm water.
- Launder as usual.
- For non-washable fabrics, remove the deposit. Then dab with a solvent or proprietary stain remover.
- Do the same for carpets. Or use carpet stain remover.
- For upholstery, use an upholstery spotting kit.

Soft Drinks

See FRUIT AND FRUIT JUICES.

Soot

- Vacuum or shake the article out of doors to get rid of as much as possible and stop it from spreading.
- Small marks will usually come out with a proprietary stain remover.
- Bad stains should be taken to a professional dry-cleaner.
- If the stain is on a carpet, begin by vacuuming. On light-coloured carpets, repeated applications of French chalk or fuller's earth should help. Rub in lightly and vacuum off when the soot has been absorbed.
- For stone and brick, see page 75.

Soup

See KETCHUP.

🔖 Spirits

- Rinse in cold water.
- Treat with methylated spirits. Rinse.
- Treat residual stains with hydrogen peroxide solution (see page 50). Rinse.
- Launder as usual.
- For non-washable fabrics, dab with lukewarm water on a sponge or absorbent cloth. Blot. Then apply lather from upholstery shampoo solution or washing-up liquid. Finally, treat with methylated spirits or a proprietary stain remover.
- For carpets, blot up the excess. Then flush with a quick squirt from a soda water siphon or sponge with a cloth wrung out in warm water. If necessary, apply carpet stain remover.
- Sponging with methylated spirits may reduce old stains.

🔖 Stove Polish (e.g. Zebrite)

- Sprinkle on salt or some other absorbent to draw up as much as possible, working it into the fabric gently with a brush.
- Repeat until most of the stain has been absorbed.
- Treat with a solvent or liquid proprietary stain remover from the wrong side.

Sweat

See PERSPIRATION.

Syrup

See JAM.

Tar

See CRUDE OIL.

 Tarnish

These stains are caused by tarnished metal such as brass, copper, tin, silver, pewter, etc.

- Dissolve the stain by flushing through from the wrong side with white vinegar or lemon juice. Rinse well with cold water.
- If the tarnish has changed the colour of the dye, sponge with household ammonia solution (see page 50) or 1 teaspoon bicarbonate of soda in ¼ pint (150 ml) warm water.
- Do not bleach.
- For non-washable fabrics, use a proprietary stain remover.

 Tea

- Flush immediately under the cold tap.
- Soak in borax solution (see page 50) or biological detergent solution if fabric allows it.
- Launder as usual.
- Soften dried stains by soaking for 1 hour in glycerine solution (equal parts glycerine and warm water), then treat as above.
- Sponge non-washable fabrics with a borax solution, then with cold water. Blot well. When dry, use a proprietary stain remover.
- For upholstery, use an upholstery spotting kit.
- For carpets, blot thoroughly while wet. Then flush with a squirt from a soda siphon and sponge with warm water. Blot well between each application. When dry, apply carpet stain remover.

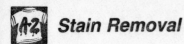

🐾 Tobacco (Nicotine Stains)

- Rinse in cold water.
- Treat with neat white vinegar. Rinse.
- Treat with liquid detergent solution (see page 50) containing 1 teaspoon methylated spirits. Rinse.
- Treat with hydrogen peroxide solution (see page 50).

🐾 Tomato Juice

See FRUIT AND FRUIT JUICES.

🐾 Transfer Patterns

- Laundering on its own may work.
- Use methylated spirits or a solvent on a cotton bud or Q-tip. Test the fabric first. (*Don't* use methylated spirits on acetate or triacetate fabrics.)

🐾 Treacle

See JAM.

🐾 Turmeric

See CURRY.

🐾 Typewriter correction fluid

- Wait until completely dry, then peel or brush off gently. Dab residue with white spirit.

💥 Unidentified Stains

- If the garment is washable, soak in cold water or a biological detergent solution.
- Wet the area and rub or spray with proprietary pre-wash product and launder as usual.
- If in doubt, take to a professional dry-cleaner.

💥 Urine

- Rinse, sponge or flush well with cold water.
- Treat with household ammonia solution (see page 50).
- Launder as usual.
- Soak dried stains in biological detergent solution if the fabric allows it. Or use a specially formulated proprietary stain remover such as De SolvIt 2 or Stain Devils Coffee and Tea Remover.
- Bleach pale-coloured and white fabrics with hydrogen peroxide solution (see page 50), with a few drops of household ammonia added.
- For non-washable fabrics, sponge with cold water immediately. Blot well. Then sponge with vinegar solution (see page 50). Dried stains should be taken to a professional dry-cleaner.
- For mattresses, turn the mattress onto its side and hold in position while treating the stain. Then press a towel below the saturated area and sponge with cold detergent solution or upholstery shampoo. Blot carefully between applications so as not to get the mattress too wet. Finally, blot with cold water with a few drops of mild antiseptic added (e.g. Dettol, Milton or pine antiseptic). It will probably be impossible to get rid of the mark completely. The important thing is to get rid of the smell and the actual urine, which could rot the fabric.
- For carpets, flush with a squirt from a soda siphon or sponge with cold water and blot well. Then sponge the

damp area with carpet shampoo. Finally, dab on several applications of cold water to which a few drops of antiseptic have been added. Don't get the carpet too wet and blot well between applications. If a dried stain has affected the dye, sponge with household ammonia solution (see page 50).

- If the stain is on a pair of shoes, soak up the urine at once with a cloth wrung out in warm water. Then polish or clean the shoes as usual. For dried stains, rub with a damp cloth from time to time as the warmth of the foot gradually drives the absorbed salts to the surface of the leather.
- Suede shoes will absorb the urine quickly so rub the marks at once with a cloth wrung out in warm water. Then brush while still damp with a suede brush. Dried marks will be very difficult to remove. Try a proprietary suede and leather stain remover.

Vaseline

See OINTMENT.

Vegetable Oil (Cooking oil, linseed oil, olive oil, etc.)

- Treat with a solvent or proprietary stain remover.
- Repeat if necessary several times.
- Saturate the fabric with cold water and treat with methylated spirits with a little white vinegar added. Rinse with cold water.
- Launder as usual.
- Treat non-washable fabrics as above but repeat the methylated spirits treatment if necessary instead of laundering.

🐾 Walnut

- Very fresh stains should be removed by boiling in hot water and detergent.
- Old stains will leave a grey colour which can only be removed with a strong solution of household bleach or hydrogen peroxide (see page 50).
- Take non-washable fabrics to a professional dry-cleaner, but don't hold out too much hope.

🐾 Watercolour Paint

See PAINT.

🐾 Wax Polish

See CAR POLISH, FURNITURE POLISH, SHOE POLISH.

🐾 Wine

- Absorb with salt.
- Rinse in warm water.
- Soak or sponge with borax solution (see page 50) or biological detergent solution if the fabric allows it.
- Launder as usual, putting a laundry stain removal sachet in with the wash.
- Dried marks on nylon or wool should be bleached with hydrogen peroxide solution (see page 50). Rinse.
- For other white fabrics, use a proprietary colour remover (such as Colour Run or Dygon) and a proprietary stain remover or a domestic bleach if the fabric has no special finish.

CAUTION

- Don't use ammonia together with bleach.

- Don't switch from one method to another before you've given the first one a chance to work.

- All fabrics can be damaged by rubbing.

- Don't try to remove stains from silk chiffon, watered silk, silk jersey or lurex – they are too fragile.

- Remember that silk and some carpet dyes are fragile and may become blotchy.

- Don't use solvents or proprietary cleaners while smoking or near any flame, even a pilot light.

- Before using any proprietary cleaner, read the manufacturer's instructions – and then follow them.

🐾 Yoghurt

- Remove the deposit with the back of a knife.
- Use a solvent or a proprietary stain remover.

🐾 Zinc and Castor Oil Ointment

- Dampen stained area. Apply white spirit and leave for few minutes. Rinse in warm water.

3

Know Your Fabrics

Most cleaning agents are perfectly safe to use on most fabrics, but there are one or two exceptions. If you are in doubt about a fabric, make sure you check that a particular cleaning agent is suitable or take it to a professional dry-cleaner.

🪰 Acetate

Man-made cellulose acetate fibre.
- Don't use acetone, acetic acid, methylated spirits or any other alcohol-based substance for stain removal.
- Bleach with hydrogen peroxide or sodium perborate solution.
- Don't use household/chlorine bleach.

🪰 Acrylic (e.g. Dralon, Acrilan, Courtelle)

Man-made fibre. May be blended with other man-made or natural fibres.
- Most cleaning agents can be used.
- Safe to use household/chlorine bleach.

✿ Angora

Very soft, fluffy rabbit wool; sometimes mixed with nylon.
- Dry-clean as for wool.
- Don't use biological detergents.
- Use hydrogen peroxide solution for bleaching.
- Don't use household/chlorine bleach.

✿ Brocade

May be acetate, cotton, silk, viscose or a mixture.
- Treat according to fibre.

✿ Camel Hair

- Treat as for wool.
- Don't use biological detergents.
- Don't use household/chlorine bleach.

✿ Cashmere

- Treat as for wool.
- Don't use biological detergents.
- Don't use household/chlorine bleach.

✿ Cavalry Twill

May be cotton, wool or man-made fibres.
- Treat according to fibre.

Stain Removal

✿ Chenille

Soft, velvety pile fabric which may be cotton, rayon, wool or silk.
- Treat according to fibre.

✿ Chiffon

May be silk, nylon, rayon or other man-made fibres.
- May be treated as a washable fabric, but with great care and tenderness.
- If silk, don't use washing soda, household/chlorine bleach or biological detergents.

✿ Chintz

Cotton furnishing fabric, often glazed.
- Treat as a washable fabric.

✿ Corduroy

May be cotton, cotton/viscose or cotton/polyester.
- Treat according to fibre.

✿ Cotton

Natural fibre made from the cotton plant.
- Can be treated as a washable fabric and boiled if necessary.
- Most cleaning agents can be used.
- Can be bleached with household/chlorine bleach.

✿ Cretonne

May be cotton or rayon. Chintz-like fabric but flimsier.
- Treat as a washable fabric.
- Use pre-wash treatment if necessary.

✿ Damask

May be cotton, linen, wool or silk.
- Treat according to fibre.

✿ Denim

Heavy cotton; sometimes cotton/viscose.
- Treat as for most delicate fibre.

✿ Dralon

See ACETATE.

✿ Elastane

Stretchy synthetic fibres.
- Always used with other fibres, so treat as for most delicate one.

✿ Felt

Matted wool material.
- Use an absorbent, such as fuller's earth, talcum powder or French chalk.
- Or make up a paste of white spirit and an absorbent

powder, rub well into the stain and allow to dry. Then brush off.
- Don't use biological detergent.
- Don't use household/chlorine bleach.

🐾 Flannel

Usually wool; may be a mixture.
- Heavy flannel should be professionally dry-cleaned.
- Lightweight flannel may be treated as wool.
- Don't use biological detergent.
- Don't use household/chlorine bleach.

🐾 Fur

- Use an absorbent, such as fuller's earth or bran, to reduce grease and surface dirt.
- Get professionally dry-cleaned periodically.

🐾 Fur Fabric

May be nylon, viscose, cotton, acrylic or polyester.
- Treat cotton and viscose as non-washable fabrics.
- Others may be treated according to care labels.
- If in doubt, treat as nylon.

🐾 Gabardine

Strong woven fabric of cotton, worsted, or blends of these and man-made fibres.
- Treat as a non-washable fabric and preferably get profesionally dry-cleaned.

Jersey

Stretchy knitted fabric of wool, silk, cotton or nylon and other man-made fibres.

- Treat according to fibre.
- If unsure of fibre, treat as a non-washable fabric.
- Don't use household/chlorine bleach.
- Don't soak in biological detergent solution.

Lace

May be cotton, nylon, polyester or a blend.

- Treat according to fibre.
- Use liquid detergent specially formulated for delicate fabrics.
- Pin to a linen-covered board with enough pins (non-rust) to keep the lace flat. Dab gently with mild detergent solution on a sponge. Sponge with clean water. Mop up as much excess water as possible.
- Acetone or a mild hydrogen peroxide or household/chlorine bleach solution may be used for difficult stains.
- Use houseold/chlorine bleach with caution. Better to use a weak solution and repeat if necessary.
- Don't soak different colours together. Oatmeal lace should not be soaked with white, for example.
- Delicate hand-made lace should be taken to an expert.

Linen

Made from fibres of the flax plant. Similar to cotton but longer-lived.

- Most treatments are safe on linen.
- Always remove stains before laundering and then use a hot wash.
- Can use household/chlorine bleach solution.

🌸 Net

May be cotton, nylon or polyester.
- Treat according to fibre.
- If curtains have gone grey, wash in proprietary whitener and then white nylon dye if necessary.
- Can be soaked in biological detergent but best to wash them before they become so dirty.
- Don't use household/chlorine bleach on nylon net.

🌸 Nylon

Man-made fibre.
- Most cleaning agents can be used safely.
- Don't boil or use a hot wash.
- Don't bleach.
- You can try a nylon whitener in the rinsing water.
- Fungicides which may help to get rid of mildew stains, are available from hardware shops. See also Fungo, page 118.

🌸 Organdie

Permanently stiffened fabric which may be cotton or nylon.
- Treat according to fibre.
- Can be given a delicate wash.

🌸 Polyester (e.g. Crimplene, Terylene, Dacron)

Man-made fibre.
- Most treatments are safe.
- Treat as a washable fabric. Don't boil.
- Badly stained articles should be impregnated with concentrated detergent. Leave for 10–15 minutes. This should loosen the stain. Launder as usual.

- Polyester/cotton sheets may become discoloured. Rub neat liquid detergent into the area and leave for 1–2 hours before rinsing.
- Put a laundry stain removal sachet in with the wash.

Rayon

See VISCOSE.

Satin

May be silk, cotton, polyester, nylon or acetate.
- Heavy furnishing satin should be professionally dry-cleaned.
- Lightweight satin may be treated as a washable fabric but with care.
- Acetate satin should not be cleaned with acetone, methylated spirits or any other alcohol-based solvent.

Sheepskin

- Take to a specialist cleaner.

Silk

Natural fibre made from the cocoon of the silk worm.
- Treat silk taffetas and brocades as non-washable fabrics.
- Silk ties should be professionally dry-cleaned.
- Washable silk garments should be washed every time they are worn to prevent perspiration stains which will weaken the fabric.
- Greasy stains can be removed with proprietary stain remover.

Stain Removal

- Other stains should be dealt with professionally. Tell the dry-cleaner what the stain consists of, if you can.
- Do not use biological detergents.
- White silk may be bleached with a hydrogen peroxide or sodium perborate solution.
- Don't use household/chlorine bleach.
- Silk can be sponged with weak household ammonia solution on the wrong side just before hand-washing.
- The colours of silk are sometimes affected by traces of alkali caused by hard water or may run during drying. To prevent this, add 2 teaspoons strong acetic acid or white vinegar to 5¼ pints (3 litres) water. After the final rinse, immerse the garment in this and leave for a few minutes. Dry without rinsing.

Straw (hats, baskets, etc.)

- Bleach stubborn marks with 1 teaspoon salt to 2 tablespoons lemon juice. Rinse in cold water. Dry in the sun.

Suede

For regular overall cleaning, take suede to a specialist cleaner. Meanwhile, there are things you can do to keep it fresh-looking.
- Clean greasy collars with a proprietary suede-cleaning cloth, available from department stores and hardware shops.
- Wear a scarf or high collar under the jacket to avoid this problem.
- A proprietary stain repellent will help to avoid stains caused by food and drink spills. Apply while coat is still new and clean.

🐾 Taffeta

May be acetate, nylon, polyester, silk, wool or viscose.
- Take to a professional dry-cleaner.
- You could try proprietary stain remover on greasy stains while still fresh.

🐾 Terylene

See POLYESTER.

🐾 Triacetate (e.g. Tricel)

Cellulose fibre made from wood pulp and cotton, often blended with other fibres.
- Take to a professional dry-cleaner.
- Don't use acetone, acetic acid, methylated spirits or any other alcohol-based solvents.

🐾 Velour

- Take to a professional dry-cleaner.

🐾 Velvet

May be cotton, nylon, silk, wool or viscose.
- Some velvets are uncrushable, spot-proof and easily washed but they do differ so make sure you find out which fibre you are dealing with and treat accordingly.
- If in doubt, take to a professional dry-cleaner.

TREATMENT FOR RAINCOATS

- Methylated or white spirit will often get rid of odd stains.
- Proofed coats can be sponged lightly with dry-cleaning solvent, but don't get them too damp.
- Reproofing and stain-repellent sprays are available from department stores. Follow the instructions. Go twice over places where the rain will fall most heavily, i.e. the shoulders.
- Add extra rain-proofing if necessary by rubbing beeswax on worn areas and pressing over brown paper. The paper will absorb excess wax, leaving enough to give protection. Don't use newspaper.

Rubberised raincoats
- Don't use dry-cleaning solvent.
- Use a paste of French chalk and water. Leave overnight.
- Or use soap flakes and water applied with a sponge or nail brush. Do not press or iron.

Plastic raincoats
- Don't use dry-cleaning solvent. Just sponge with soapy water and rinse well. Dry away from heat.

🐾 Viscose

Cellulose-based fibre.
- Treat as a washable fabric, but don't rub, twist or wring.
- Do not use acetone, acetic acid, methylated spirits or any other alcohol-based solvent.

🐾 Wool

Natural fibre from sheep, goats or camel family.
- Use liquid detergent and never rub while wet.
- Some wools are now treated so as to be machine-washable and they may be treated as washable fabrics.
- Most wool should be treated as non-washable.
- Don't use biological detergents.
- Always dry wool away from sunlight or direct heat.
- Don't use household/chlorine bleach.
- Yellowed white wool can be soaked in 1 part hydrogen peroxide to 10 parts water. Just squeeze gently. Never use water hotter than lukewarm.
- Don't rub, twist or wring while wet.

4

*H*ousehold *S*tain *R*emoval

🐾 Acrylic

- Rub marks or scratches with metal polish.
- Don't use abrasives.
- See also BATHS.

🐾 Alabaster

See MARBLE.

🐾 Aluminium

Cooking Pans

- To remove discolouration after boiling water, boil a weak solution of acid (water plus lemon skins, apple peels or rhubarb), rinse and dry.
- Soaking in a borax solution (see page 50) may remove acid stains.

Teapots

- Use bicarbonate of soda on a damp cloth to remove tea stains.
- Or use a borax solution (see page 50).

Bamboo

See CANE.

Baths

Acrylic

- Remove light marks and scratches by rubbing gently with silver polish.

Fibreglass

- Use nothing but a soft cloth and mild detergent; no abrasives.

Vitreous and Porcelain Enamel

- Use a non-abrasive bathroom or all-purpose household cleaner such as Oz.
- Or simply use neat white vinegar or lemon juice. Both are good for removing hard water scale.
- Never use harsh abrasives.

Blankets

- Treat according to fibre.
- Electric blankets should regularly be sent back to the

Stain Removal

manufacturer for servicing. Don't try to tackle stains at home.

🐾 Blinds

Canvas

- Scrub stained patches on washable blinds with warm detergent solution. Rinse well. Dry naturally.
- For lightly stained spots, use a soft eraser.
- Or use a proprietary stain remover.

Venetian

- Use detergent solution. Put on fabric gloves; dip your fingers in the solution and rub the marked slat between finger and thumb.
- For fly spots, dip your gloved fingers in cold tea (without milk).

🐾 Books

- Remove grease spots by putting some tissues on either side of the page and pressing gently with a warm iron.
- Fresh mildew can be wiped off with a soft dry cloth. Or dust the pages with cornflour, French chalk or unperfumed talc. Leave for several days, then brush out with a clean make-up or watercolour paint brush.
- If the book is precious or antique, consult a professional conservator.

🐾 Brass

- If very dirty, wash in household ammonia solution (see page 50).

- Clean with neat white vinegar and salt or half a lemon. Wash carefully and polish with an essential oil (from chemists and herb shops) on a soft cloth.
- Or use a proprietary metal polish.
- Very dirty objects such as fire tongs may be rubbed with steel wool or very fine emery cloth. Rub up and down, not round and round. It's a long job. Afterwards wash thoroughly in hot water and detergent.

Bricks

- Efflorescence (a white deposit) should be washed repeatedly with water. Allow to dry between applications.
- Or brush the wall with a stiff bristle or wire brush.
- Sponge oily stains with white spirit.
- Wearing gloves, cover graffiti with paint stripper; then wash with soapy water.
- Smoky marks should be rubbed with an art gum eraser or scrubbed with neat liquid detergent.
- Soot should be vacuumed first and then treated as above.

Bronze

- Try not to touch the surface except to dust lightly with a soft clean duster once or twice a year. Abrasives will damage the surface.
- Antique bronzes should be taken to an expert.
- Never wash valuable or antique bronze. This can cause rapid corrosion and the metal may start flaking away.
- Don't use methylated spirits or solvents on bronze.
- Remove verdigris by rubbing with a toothbrush.
- For not very valuable but very dirty pieces, wash with a soft brush in very hot detergent solution. Rinse, dry and buff up.

Stain Removal

Cane/Bamboo/Wicker/Rattan

- Rub with mild detergent solution with a few drops of household ammonia added. Dry thoroughly.
- Polish with furniture cream if necessary.

China/Porcelain/Pottery

- Make cracks in fine porcelain less obvious by removing the dirt. Cove the crack with a cotton wool pad soaked in a household ammonia or household bleach solution (see page 50). Leave for several days, wetting the pad from time to time with more solution. Scrub gently if necessary with a fine bristle brush dipped in the solution.
- Rub tea and coffee stains with a soft wet cloth dipped in bicarbonate of soda. Proprietary products exist but bicarbonate of soda is cheaper.
- Very fine or antique porcelain should be taken to a professional conservator.

Chrome

- Remove greasy marks and fly spots with a little paraffin on a damp cloth.
- Never use abrasives.
- Treat corrosion with a metal cleaner or chrome cleaner (from car accessory shops or hardware stores).

Concrete floors

- Remove oil by scrubbing with a strong solution of household detergent. Remove residue with white spirit, if necessary.

🐾 Continental Quilts

See DUVETS.

🐾 Copper

- Remove corroded spots with neat white vinegar; lemon juice and salt; buttermilk; or a proprietary copper cleaner. Rinse and dry well.
- Equal parts salt, vinegar and flour make a satisfactory copper polish.

Cooking Pans

- Copper saucepans should have their exteriors cleaned as above. They are always lined with either tin or nickel because copper reacts badly to certain foods and from time to time the lining should be renewed.
- For burned-on food, soak in water. Then use a nylon scourer or nylon brush.

🐾 Cork

- Sponge gently with warm mild detergent solution.
- Don't get it very wet.
- Rub black marks with an eraser.

🐾 Decanters and Vases

- Fill with household ammonia solution (see page 50) and leave overnight. Wash and rinse.
- Shake tea leaves and vinegar around in a vase to get rid of the stains and silt at the bottom. Leave to stand for a while, then rinse and dry. Repeat if necessary.

Stain Removal

- Or fill the base with small ball bearings and rattle them around gently.
- Alternatively, use a little sea sand or fine aquarium gravel in a detergent solution. Shake well, leave to soak, shake again. Rinse and repeat if necessary. This should get rid of flower and plant debris and wine sediment.
- Or you could fill the receptacle with proprietary cleaner, leave to soak, then rinse out.
- A bottle brush will help you get into corners.

🌼 Duvets

- Follow the manufacturer's care instructions.
- Always keep a removable cover on duvets and treat according to fibre.
- If the duvet itself becomes stained, consult a specialist cleaner.

🌼 Electric Irons

- Remove dried starch with a damp cloth while the iron is slightly warm.
- Clean the sole plate with metal polish.
- Remove melted synthetics by gently heating until soft and removing with a plastic or wooden spatula or other implement which won't scratch the base plate. Don't use a metal knife.
- You can use very fine steel wool for stubborn marks but be careful not to damage the sole plate.
- Scaled-up steam irons can be cleaned with a proprietary de-scaler, such as Descalite, available from chemists.

🌼 Emulsion Paint

See WALLS.

🐝 Enamel

- If food is burned on, soak for a few hours in cold water.
- You can safely use a nylon scouring pad, not a metal one.
- For badly burned-on food, fill the pan with water plus two teaspoons bicarbonate of soda and boil.
- Light stains can be removed with a damp cloth dipped in bicarbonate of soda.

🐝 Frames

Gilt

- Wipe with a little white spirit or turpentine or dry-cleaning solvent.

Wood

- Wipe with a cloth wrung out in warm detergent solution.

🐝 Freezers

See REFRIGERATORS AND FREEZERS.

🐝 Garage Floors

See CONCRETE FLOORS.

🐝 Glass

- Badly stained cut glass or glass which has become cloudy can be left to soak for several hours in warm water with a few drops of household ammonia added.

Stain Removal

- Scratched glass surfaces should be rubbed lightly with a chamois leather impregnated with jeweller's rouge.
- Fly spots on glass can be cleaned with white vinegar and water or neat vinegar.

Gold and Gilt

- Don't touch the surface except to dust it lightly with a clean dry duster or chamois leather. Ordinary cloths may harbour tiny particles of grit which could damage the metal.
- Clean tarnished low-carat gold with a long-term silver polish.
- When not in use, wrap in chamois leather or acid-free tissue.
- Antique or precious gold should be taken to a jeweller.

Iron

- Remove rust by rubbing with steel wool dipped in paraffin. If the item is small enough, soak it in paraffin for 1–2 hours, then rub with steel wool. Work outside and don't work near a naked flame.
- Use a rust inhibitor, such as Movol, to prevent rust from forming again.
- Rub large objects (such as fences, gates, furniture, etc.) with a wire brush. Wipe over the surface with white spirit on a cloth. Don't use water or the rust will return.

Ivory

- Bleach yellowed ivory by rubbing it with a little neat hydrogen peroxide. Leave it in the sun to dry.
- Treat old glue stains with a stiff paste of whiting and

hydrogen peroxide. Cover the stain and wait until the paste is dry. Wipe off the paste and dry thoroughly with a soft, clean cloth.

- Almond oil on a soft rag will give a protective coating for the future.
- If the ivory is valuable, get professional advice.

🐾 Laminated Plastic

- Don't use abrasives, chemical cleaners or ammonia.
- Rub light stains with a damp cloth dipped in bicarbonate of soda.
- Wipe stubborn stains with toothpaste or cover in a paste of bicarbonate of soda and water and leave for several hours. Rub briskly before wiping off.

🐾 Lampshades

- Kitchen shades, which get particularly dirty and greasy, can be cleaned with a strong detergent such as carpet shampoo.
- Clean other shades according to fabric.
- Get silk lampshades professionally cleaned.

🐾 Lavatories

- Remove hard water scale by leaving tissues soaked in neat white vinegar round the marks for a few minutes, then brush hard with a lavatory brush.
- For general stains, first push the water down the drain by wrapping the lavatory brush in an old cloth or towel and 'plunging' several times. Apply a paste of borax and lemon juice to the stains. Leave for 1–2 hours, then scrub clean.

Stain Removal

- Or use bleach.
- Or use a proprietary lavatory cleaner such as Harpic.
- Do *not* mix bleach and lavatory cleaner or any two cleaning agents together.

Lead

- Scrub with turpentine or white spirit.
- Remove white deposits by boiling in several changes of water.
- Place very dirty objects in a solution of 1 part white vinegar to 9 parts water with 1 teaspoon bicarbonate of soda. Rinse in several changes of distilled water.

Marble

- Badly stained marble is difficult to treat. Get the advice of an antique dealer if the piece is valuable.
- Wipe up spills as quickly as possible to prevent them staining.
- Solvents such as methylated spirits, acetone, lighter fuel and proprietary cleaners can be used.
- Deep stains can be treated by making a paste of solvent and whiting (from chemists). Leave this on the stain for several hours, before wiping off gently. Repeat if necessary.
- For rust stains, use a paste made with a commercial rust remover (see address on page 117).
- Remove organic stains made by such things as coloured paper, leaves, tobacco, tea, coffee and cosmetics with neat hydrogen peroxide applied directly. Add 1–2 drops household ammonia and leave until the bubbling stops. Rinse with water.
- For ink stains, treat as above or apply a hydrogen peroxide solution (see page 50) and rinse off after a few minutes.

- Don't allow marble to get too wet or to remain wet after treatment.
- Minor scratches can usually be removed by patient rubbing with powdered tin oxide (putty powder) available from hardware stores. Sprinkle the powder on the surface and rub vigorously with a moistened chamois.
- Very dirty marble can be treated with Bell Marble Cleaner (see address on page 116).

🐾 Melamine

- Melamine stains rather easily but you can remove stubborn stains with a little toothpaste rubbed on with an old toothbrush or a damp cloth.
- Don't use scouring powders or pads.
- Bicarbonate of soda will remove light stains.
- Soaking in sodium perborate solution (see page 103) is usually effective for heavy stains.

🐾 Metals

See ALUMINIUM, BRASS, BRONZE, CHROME, COPPER, GOLD, IRON, LEAD, PEWTER, SILVER, STAINLESS STEEL and TIN.

🐾 Mirrors

- Clean fly spots and bathroom splashes with neat white vinegar or cold tea (without milk).

🐾 Oil-Based Paint

See WALL COVERINGS.

Stain Removal

Paint

See WALL COVERINGS.

Perspex

See ACRYLIC.

Pewter

- If it is kept in a humid atmosphere, pewter will quickly develop a 'hume', with a grey film and tarnishing.
- Ordinary pewter can be polished with a suitable proprietary metal polish or with whiting and a little househould ammonia. Don't do this more than two or three times a year.
- Or rub with raw cabbage leaves or the green part of a raw leek.
- Antique or valuable pewter should always be dealt with by a professional conservator.

Porcelain

See CHINA.

Pots and Pans

Aluminium

See ALUMINIUM.

Cast Iron Pans

- For burned-on food, fill the pan with water and 1 table-spoon liquid washing soda or washing soda crystals and boil. Rinse.
- Remove rust with steel wool and an abrasive cleaner.
- Don't use detergents.
- Don't store pans with their lids on.

Enamel Pans

- Burned-on grease should be soaked in hot water and detergent (*not* washing soda). Use a washing-up brush or nylon scourer, not a metal one.

Glass Pans

- Remove burned-on food with bicarbonate of soda on a damp cloth.
- Or use a proprietary ceramic hob cleaner such as Easy-Do Cleaner Conditioner.

Non-Stick Pans

- For stubborn stains, mix ¼ pint (150 ml) water, 2 table-spoons bicarbonate of soda and 3 fl oz (75 ml) household bleach and boil up in the pan for 5–10 minutes.
- Don't use abrasives.

Roasting Tins

- If a baking or roasting tin has a lot of baked-on grease, soak it for about half an hour in 1 pint (600 ml) very hot water poured over 1 dessertspoon washing soda crystals. Scrub with a nylon scourer. Rinse well.
- Less stubborn marks can be removed with a damp cloth dipped in bicarbonate of soda.

Stain Removal

🐾 Pottery

See CHINA.

🐾 Quarry Tiles

- White patches should be washed with 1 tablespoon white vinegar to 1 pint (600 ml) hot water. Don't rinse. Repeat if necessary from time to time.

🐾 Rattan

See CANE.

🐾 Refrigerators and Freezers

- For exterior stains, use warm detergent solution.
- For interior stains, use bicarbonate of soda on a damp cloth.
- Don't use abrasives and always dry well after cleaning.

🐾 Silver

- Silver needs constant care. Always wash it as soon as possible after use in hot water and detergent.
- Clean tarnished silver with a proprietary silver polish such as Goddards.
- Dip cleaners like Johnson's Silver Dip are suitable for cutlery. If you can't get the object into the jar, dab it with cotton wool saturated with the cleaner. Don't leave silver in the jar longer than necessary.
- A soft toothbrush is useful to get into chased surfaces.
- Wash thoroughly because any traces of polish will cause the silver to tarnish more quickly.

PREVENTION OF TARNISH IS BETTER THAN CURE

- Never use rubber bands to secure wrappings round silver.
- To store silver, use special bags, wraps and rolls of cloth which have been impregnated with tarnish inhibitor (see address on page 117).
- Salt, eggs, olives, salad dressings, vinegar, fruit juices and perfumes all have a tarnishing effect on silver.
- Acids from decaying flowers will tarnish silver quickly.

🐾 Slate

- Use washing soda solution.
- For greasy stains, use a dry-cleaning solvent. Repeat if necessary.
- As a finishing treatment, wipe over with a cloth dipped in milk to give a matt shine.

🐾 Sports Shoes

- Allow any mud to dry and then brush off thoroughly.
- Clean with soap or detergent solution.
- Treat white shoes with a special white cleaner or whiting powder (from chemists) mixed to a paste with water.

🐾 Stainless Steel

- Remove water spots on sinks and draining boards with neat white vinegar or methylated spirits. Wipe dry at once.

Stain Removal

- Don't use abrasives, scouring pads, salt, vinegar, steel wool or detergent powder for cleaning.
- Shine the inside and outside of a pan by rubbing with half a lemon or neat white vinegar on a cloth.
- Don't use metal scourers or scouring powders.
- If an item is very dirty, just soak in warm soapy water.

Taps

- Remove lime scale with half a lemon. Rub this over the scaly parts and leave for a few minutes, then wipe off with a clean cloth.
- Or soak cotton wool or tissues in neat white vinegar and leave wrapped round the scaly parts for a few minutes. Wipe with a clean cloth.
- A few drops of paraffin on a damp cloth will get rid of water marks and leave the taps shining.

Tin

- Remove rust with a potato dipped in mild abrasive cleaning powder. Rinse well.

Vacuum Flasks

- Coffee and tea stains can be removed by shaking crushed eggshells and hot water inside. Leave for half an hour, then rinse.
- For other stains, fill with warm water and 1 tablespoon bicarbonate of soda. Leave for 2–3 hours, then rinse.

Vinyl Flooring

- For scuff marks, use a soft eraser or emulsion floor polish.

- Don't use paraffin, lighter fuel, white spirit or any other solvent and don't use wax polish.

Wall Coverings

- Dab ballpoint pen with methylated spirits.
- Rub crayon and felt-tip pen colours with all-purpose cleaner.

Emulsion and Eggshell Paint

- Rub with mild detergent solution or all-purpose cream cleaner.
- If working near electric switches, sockets or plugs, turn electricity off at the mains.

Expanded Polystyrene

- Sponge with warm mild detergent solution.
- Don't apply pressure.
- Allow to dry thoroughly.

Fabric

- Dab greasy stains with talcum powder, fuller's earth or some other absorbent. Leave for 1–2 hours. Brush off with a soft brush.
- Don't use dry-cleaning solvent, stain removers or upholstery or carpet shampoo.

Grasscloth and Hessian

- Dab greasy stains with talcum powder or some other absorbent. Leave for 1–2 hours. Brush off with a soft brush or use a proprietary stain remover.

Stain Removal

Oil-Based Paint

- Use a mild detergent solution or an all-purpose cream cleaner.

Silk Wallhangings

- Consult a specialist dry-cleaner.

 Wallpaper

Embossed Papers

- Dab greasy marks with talcum powder. Leave for a few hours, then brush off with a soft brush. Or use a proprietary stain remover.
- Clean general stains with mild detergent solution or an all-purpose household cleaner. Don't get the paper too wet. The dab and blot technique is best (see page 12).

Washable

- Even if it's washable it's best not to get any wallpaper too wet, and you should always test an unobtrusive bit first.
- Draw out greasy stains, including candle wax, with a warm iron over blotting paper or tissues held over the stain. Or rub gently with a damp cloth dipped in bicarbonate of soda.
- Remove lipstick with a dry-cleaning solvent or proprietary stain remover.
- Remove sticky tape and draw out the residual mark using the blotting paper and warm iron method described for greasy stains.
- Clean general stains with a bread ball, used like an eraser. Or use a soft eraser.

🦋 Wicker

See CANE.

🦋 Windows

- Fresh paint can be rubbed off with turpentine, solvent or non-oily nail varnish remover.
- Dry paint should be softened with turpentine and then scraped off.
- Putty should be softened with turpentine, as for dried paint. Or you could use a household ammonia solution (see page 50).
- Remove sticky label adhesive with methylated spirits.
- Don't use a dry cloth.
- Don't use soap.

🦋 Wood

- Remove finger marks by rubbing briskly with a soft cloth.
- See box on pages 93–94 for various remedial treatments for wood.

Carved Wood

- Get into corners with a paint brush.

French-Polished Furniture

- Dust with a paint brush.
- If alcohol is spilled on the surface, it will remove the polish. Wipe up the spill immediately and rub the area with the palm of your hand. This is slightly oily and will help to replace the wax.

Stain Removal

- Remove any build-up of old wax polish with neat white vinegar on a damp cloth.
- Greasy marks can be removed with a chamois wrung out in a mixture of 1 tablespoon white vinegar in ½ pint (300 ml) cold water.
- Apply polish only about twice a year.

Gilded Finishes

- Remove stains by gently dabbing with half a raw onion.
- Don't try to retouch any true gilding at home. Get professional advice.
- Never touch up gilding with gold paint, which is a different material and a different colour.

Untreated Wood (e.g. worktops and tables)

- Scrub with scouring powder.
- Then rub in a little teak or linseed oil.

Wooden Floors: Painted

- Rub with liquid detergent solution.
- Or use a handful of washing soda crystals in a bucket of hot water. Don't scrub.

Wooden Floors: Varnished

- Rub marks with cold tea (without milk).

Wooden Floors: Waxed

- Most marks on waxed wood can be removed by rubbing with mild detergent solution.
- For stubborn stains, use fine steel wool dipped in liquid wax polish.

- Treat white spots and rings with wood ash and raw potato or salad oil or mayonnaise.
- Don't get the floor too wet.

Wooden Garden Furniture

- Rub gently with fine wire wool or a nylon scourer in the direction of the grain to remove lichen and weather stains.
- Don't scrub or use abrasives.

REMEDIAL TREATMENTS FOR WOOD

If the piece is antique or valuable, take it to a professional.

Black Water Marks
- Rub the surface with a very fine grade steel wool then re-colour with a proprietary wood stain and polish.
- Or bleach with a proprietary wood bleach like A. Sanderson's.
- If the piece is antique, get professional advice.

Cigarette Burns
- Treat as for white rings.
- If necessary, lightly sandpaper the area and build it up again with coloured beeswax or wax crayon.
- If the piece is antique, get professional advice.

Ink Stains
- Try a proprietary wood bleach such as A. Sanderson's. Follow the instructions carefully and remember little and often is better than over-bleaching in a single treatment.

Scratch Marks

- Rub with the broken surface of a Brazil nut kernel.
- Rub with proprietary furniture renovator like Topps Scratch Cover Polish, working in the direction of the grain.
- Pour on cod liver oil or linseed oil and leave to soak in. Wipe off excess.

White Frosting

- This is sometimes the result of a damp environment. It may cover the whole surface but is unlikely to penetrate the wood.
- Dip a piece of fine steel wool into cooking oil and rub in the direction of the grain. Finish off with a wax polish.

White Ring Marks

- Don't try to remove ring marks caused by water until the water has dried out completely.
- If you leave them alone, the light and the temperature of the room may cause the rings to fade away completely.
- When dried, if the rings still remain, cover them with a paste of salt and olive oil. Leave on the mark overnight. Remove and polish the wood as usual. Repeat if necessary.
- Or apply a paste of cigarette ash and olive oil as above.
- Or apply mayonnaise as above.
- Or rub with metal polish in the direction of the grain. Buff up with a soft cloth.

5

*P*revention is *B*etter than *C*ure

Although modern chemicals and up-to-date techniques can help remove many stains, there are many substances which will stain permanently even if dealt with while fresh. If you can prevent things being spilled in the first place, or at least from being absorbed, fabrics and furniture will remain in good condition for much longer. Here are some simple precautions.

General

- Wear an apron or old clothes while cooking, painting, gardening or doing any other potentially dirty jobs.
- Wear overalls if working on car, bike, motorbike or lawn mower.
- Lay a very big door mat by outside doors. Matting can be bought by the metre and prevents mud and tar from spreading through the house from shoes.
- Make sure children (and careless adults) eat at the dining table so they won't spill food and drink on the best carpet.
- Paint at least one wall in a child's room with washable

paint so children can legitimately chalk or crayon all over it and leave the rest of the house alone.

- When changing the toner in a printer, or using inks or paints, cover the working area with newspaper so any spillages will not go on the floor.
- Check that candles are firmly in their holders and not leaning drunkenly over the tablecloth.
- Thorough rinsing and starching of clothes will help to prevent dirt reattaching itself to a fabric.
- Spray-on fabric protectors (e.g. 3M) will help to prevent spills being absorbed into upholstery and carpets.
- Keep shoes polished to prevent water and other stains from being absorbed.
- After every cooking session wipe hob and oven with a damp cloth dipped in bicarbonate of soda to prevent food becoming encrusted.
- When opening bottles, jars and tins of any kind, make sure you do it over a smooth, wipable surface and not over a carpet or tablecloth.
- Prevent colours running in the wash by always washing whites separately, and using a cool wash programme for coloureds.
- When using make-up, protect your clothes by wearing a scarf over your shoulders.
- When house painting, cover the floor and all furniture with dust sheets or polythene sheeting and wipe off excess paint as you go.
- Make sure animals have access to the outside through a cat flap, or walk them frequently, or see that the litter tray is easily accessible and frequently emptied and cleaned to prevent urine stains.

Floors

- Use a cement sealer on concrete floors so they won't

absorb stains. It will also make them easier to sweep and wash.

- Use a cement sealer and wax polish to protect stone floors.
- Use a sealer or wax polish on linoleum floors to make them resistant to stains (not on vinyl floors).
- Use a sealer or varnish to protect cork floors.

6

A Guide to Cleaning Agents

 Abrasives

Whiting

A finely ground chalk used as an abrasive. There are three grades: Spanish white, gilder's white, and Paris white, which is the finest.
- Non-poisonous.
- Available from hardware stores.

Absorbents

Bran is a good substance for absorbing grit and greasy dirt from fur, felt and other fabrics which should not be washed. Its non-slippery qualities help it to remain in the fabric and it cleans rather in the way a dry shampoo cleans hair.

Cornflour, French chalk, fuller's earth, oatmeal and talcum powder are all useful absorbents and can be used in the same way as bran.

Salt will absorb urine, wine and fruit juice from table linen and carpets.

Terry towelling is an excellent absorbent. It should be white and clean.

Tissues are good on carpets and robust fabrics. Professional dry-cleaners would prefer you not to use them on garments you take to be cleaned.

Acids

These can counteract the colour change caused when an alkali spills on a fabric.

Acetic Acid

A colourless liquid used to revive blue and brighter coloured fabrics by rinsing away alkaline hard water residues. (White vinegar is a form of acetic acid and can be used just as well.) Acetic acid will neutralise any alkali effects on silk and improve the lustre.

- Dilute, using 1 tablespoon to 1 bucket of water.
- Available from chemists.

Citric Acid (Lemon Juice)

- Use as acetic acid.
- A squeeze or two in the rinsing water can help to brighten colours, especially in hard water areas.

Oxalic Acid

This is one of the strongest organic acids; it is found in wood sorrel (*oxalis*) and rhubarb leaves. Oxalic acid can be used for cleaning brassware and for ink and rust stains.

- Dissolve 1 teaspoon oxalic acid crystals in ½ pint (300 ml) warm water. Make up in a glass or china dish because it will damage metal.

Stain Removal

- Test for colour-fastness (see page 9) before using on nylon and viscose.
- Rinse well with water.
- Poisonous. Label clearly.
- Wear protective gloves. Keep out of reach of children.
- Available from chemists.

White Vinegar

See ACETIC ACID.

 ## Alkalis

These will help to counteract the colour change caused when an acid such as wine spills on a fabric.

Ammonia

A colourless gas which dissolves in water to form an alkali and grease solvent. Do *not* use on silk, wool, aluminium or sisal.
- Poisonous.
- Wear rubber gloves and don't get on skin or in eyes.
- Available from chemists and hardware stores.

Bicarbonate of Soda (Sodium Bicarbonate)

A powdered substance used in baking, which will remove stains from china, glass, tiles, teeth, chrome, ovens, refrigerators and worktops.
- Apply with a damp cloth.
- Non-poisonous.
- Available from chemists, grocers and supermarkets.

Borax

This is a mild alkali which is safe on most fabrics.
- A solution can be sponged onto the garment or used for soaking (see page 50).
- Soak for 10–15 minutes only or the fabric may lose some colour.

Sodium Carbonate (Washing Soda, Soda Crystals)

Useful as a water softener and varnish remover and for cleaning drains. Do *not* use on aluminium, silk, wool, sisal or vinyl.
- Wear gloves or use a greasy hand cream before handling.
- Available as crystals or liquid from chemists, ironmongers and supermarkets. Follow manufacturer's instructions.

Sodium Hexametaphosphate (e.g. Calgon)

This is a water softener which is gentler than washing soda.
- Use as washing soda.
- Dissolves easily.
- Available from chemists and department stores. Not often found in supermarkets because it is expensive.

Sodium Hypochlorite (Household Bleach or Chlorine Bleach)

See under BLEACHES.

Sodium Perborate

See under BLEACHES.

Sodium Sesquicarbonate

A powdery water softener which dissolves easily and is milder than washing soda and cheaper than Calgon.

Stain Removal

- Use as washing soda.
- Available from chemists.

Sodium Thiosulphate ('Hypo')

- Can be used to remove chlorine and iodine stains on all fibres. Won't alter colours.
- Available from chemists and photographic suppliers.

 Bleaches

Colour Removers

These are proprietary products which remove colours from fabrics you want to dye or which have been washed with articles of another colour and taken on some of the colour. They include Colour Run and Dygon. Follow manufacturer's instructions.

Household Bleach or Chlorine Bleach (Sodium Hypochlorite)

Household or chlorine bleach will remove many stains from baths, sinks, enamelware, tiles and woodwork.

It can be used, diluted, as a bleach for white cottons, linens and synthetics (see dilution chart on page 50).

Do *not* use on silk, wool, mohair, leather, elastane or resin-treated fabrics.

- Always test for colour-fastness first (see page 9) and don't leave the article for longer than 15 minutes.
- Use in a very weak solution on coloured linens and cottons to remove stains.
- Even cotton and linen fibres will weaken if left in household bleach too long.
- Soak washable fabrics in a mild bleach solution for 5–15 minutes. Rinse thoroughly.
- *Never* mix household bleach with other cleaners.

Hydrogen Peroxide

A mild and slow-acting disinfectant and bleach, *not* to be used on nylon or flame-resistant fabrics. But, unlike other bleaches, it can be used on silk.

- A solution that is too strong or used for too long will attack organic material such as clothing or human skin.
- Available from chemists in a dilute solution, usually 20 times its own volume of water (20 vol). When used as a laundry bleach on white articles it should be further diluted with water (see page 50).
- If you add ½ teaspoon household ammonia to 1¾ pints (1 litre) hydrogen peroxide solution, it will speed up the bleaching process, but don't do this if the fabric contains wool or silk.
- To apply hydrogen peroxide to a specific stain, rather than the whole article, apply with a medicine dropper directly onto the stain, and work from the wrong side. Hold a pad of tissues under the stain. Keep adding more bleach until the stain disappears.
- Never put any peroxide back into the bottle.

Sodium Perborate

This is a soft bleach for all fabrics but don't use a hot solution on heat-sensitive fabrics such as wool or synthetics.

- When using proprietary preparations, follow the manufacturer's instructions.
- Use china or glass containers, not metal.
- Test for colour-fastness first (see page 9).
- For washable fabrics, dissolve 1–2 tablespoons in 1 pint (600 ml) hot water. Soak for several hours, as this is a slow-working bleach.
- If a fabric becomes yellowed by the solution, sponge it well with acetic acid or neat white vinegar and rinse well.
- Non-washable fabrics may be sprinkled with sodium perborate and covered with a cotton wool pad dampened

with water. Keep the pad damp until the stain has disappeared.
- Use hot water if possible, and cool water only on heat-sensitive fabrics.
- Pure sodium perborate crystals can be bought from chemists.

🐾 Detergents

These dissolve easily in hard water without the need for water softeners. They are useful for rubbing neat into greasy stains or for soaking dried stains on washable fabrics.

Biological (Enzyme) Detergents

Good for soaking protein stains such as blood, egg, gravy, etc.
- These detergents should be dissolved in warm, not hot, water and the article soaked for 12 hours or so.

Washing-Up Liquid

A mild detergent suitable for use on washable fabrics.

Other Useful Detergents

Hand-wash detergents, such as Stergene, Travel Wash, Woolite and so on, can be used in the same way as washing-up liquid.

🐾 Disinfectants

On the whole these are not stain removers, but they will help to prevent certain stains from spreading and will diminish the smell from such stains as urine and vomit. They are useful for dealing with mildew as well. Mild disinfectants include Milton, Dettol and general household disinfectants. Household (chlorine) bleach and hydrogen peroxide are disinfectants as well as bleaches.

🐾 Lubricating Agents

Eucalyptus Oil

• Use as glycerine.
• Available from chemists.

Glycerine

Good for grass stains and oil and can help to 'slide' chewing gum out of hair.
• Use to lubricate and soften certain substances in order to work them out of the fabric.
• Available from chemists.

Margarine, Vaseline and Lard

• Use as glycerine.

🐾 Proprietary Stain Removal Products

These are proprietary products similar to solvents but often with added ingredients. Some are general-purpose stain removers; others are specially formulated to deal with specific stains.

Stain Removal

Carpet and Upholstery Stain Removers and Spotting Kits

Foamy detergents which don't make the fabric too wet. Very effective on new spills and good on most dried stains as well.
- Follow manufacturer's instructions.
- Available from department stores, hardware stores and supermarkets.

General Stain Removers

These include Dabitoff, K2r and Boots Stain Remover. They will remove many stains, but it is important to follow the manufacturer's instructions.

Hand Cleaners

These include Swarfega which will remove oily and grassy substances from the skin.

In-Wash Treatments

These include Glo White Stain Remover, in sachets. Put one sachet in with each wash. It can be used in a hot or cool wash.

They work in a similar way to pre-wash treatments, lightening white fabrics and bringing out the colours in coloured ones. They are especially effective if the stain is still fresh, but they do work on many dried stains as well.

Pet Stain Removers

These include such products as Savvy, Pet Stain Remover and Lift Off. They are absorbent products containing a deodorant and can be used for urine or liquid spills such as wine.

Pre-wash Treatments

These include spray-on products such as Friend, squeeze-on products such as Ecover Stain Remover or rub-on products such as Vanish. They break down heavily stained areas on washable fabrics and loosen ingrained dirt so that it comes out in the wash.

Pre-wash treatments should work on dye, paint, ink, rust or blood, though they may make old, dried blood stains less obvious rather than get rid of them completely.

Soap-Like Bars

These include Vanish. Can be used on carpets and upholstery, as a pre-wash treatment or on all sorts of stains, particularly greasy ones.

Stain Removers Formulated for Specific Stains

These include DeSolvIt 1 and DeSolvIt 2, each formulated to deal with a particular range of stains. DeSolvIt 1 is a stain remover and pre-wash treatment which will remove grease, tar, gum, shoe polish, crayon, oil and wet paint. DeSolvIt 2 will deal with coffee, soup, wine, fruit juices, sauces, grass and blood.

They also include Stain Devils: 13 products for specific stains which between them will deal with nearly every eventuality. It's an expensive way to do it when one or two non-proprietary products can do the trick, but one or two of those you most often require, or which will get rid of difficult stains like ink and iron mould, would be useful.

🐾 Solvents

These are liquids which will dissolve grease, oils and fats.

Stain Removal

Acetone

A solvent for animal and vegetable oils, nail varnish and paint.
- Will dissolve acetate and triacetate fabrics.
- Very flammable.
- Available from chemists.

Amyl Acetate

A solvent for celluloid and cellulose paint. Also used in nail varnish removers and in some paint removers.
- Poisonous; highly flammable. Don't breathe the fumes and keep windows open while working.
- Available from chemists.

Methylated Spirits

Dissolves essential oils, castor oil, shellac, some dyes, ballpoint pen ink, iodine, grass stains and some medicines. Also useful for cleaning mirrors and glass objects.
- Poisonous; highly flammable.
- Available from chemists and hardware shops.

Professional Dry-Cleaning Solvents

Various solvents are used by professional dry-cleaners, among them solvent 11, white spirit and perchloroethylene.
- On the care label the symbol 'A' in a circle means that all solvents usually used for dry-cleaning are safe on the garment.
- On the care label the symbol 'P' in a circle means the article can be cleaned with solvent 11, white spirit or perchloroethylene.
- On the care label the symbol 'P' with a line under it means that all the above solvents may be used but with

certain restrictions as to adding water, the mechanical action and the drying temperatures.

Turpentine

Balsam made from pine trees. Used as a solvent in some paints, varnishes and waxes.
- Always use true turpentine when specified, as there is no real substitute.
- Dries out the hands so put on greasy hand cream after use or wear rubber gloves and wash them afterwards.
- Poisonous; flammable.
- Available from chemists and paint shops.

White Spirit

A colourless solvent made from mineral oils used as thinners for paints. A general-purpose grease and stain remover.
- Dries out the hands so put on greasy hand cream after use or wear rubber gloves and wash them afterwards.
- Poisonous; flammable.

7

*G*etting the *B*est from *D*ry-*C*leaners

What Dry-Cleaning Does

Although water is one of the best and most useful cleaners available, it can shrink and distort some fibres such as wool and silk. It can also make certain dyes run, and if there is any doubt about a fibre or a fabric it is better to get the article dry-cleaned.

Dry-cleaning involves the use of solvents to remove dirt and stains from fabrics. It is called dry-cleaning because the solvents used have little or no water added to them.

Inevitably some stains persist and require specialised treatment to remove them. This treatment, known as 'spotting', is the most skilled professional dry-cleaning operation available. An old stain may be impossible to remove and a good dry-cleaner should be able to tell you this.

Steam-pressing is a restorative treatment used to return clothes to their original shape, replace permanent creases and eliminate wrinkles. Stream-pressing must be done by skilled people, and information on new fabrics and special processes and temperatures suitable for their treatment is continually being issued to cleaners.

110

Certain articles are best taken to a specialist company and these include suede, leather and duvets or continental quilts.

Special Services

Many dry-cleaners will do small repairs and alterations.

Replacement of buttons may be included in the overall cleaning charge or there may be a small extra charge.

Retexturing impregnates fabrics with a dressing which renews the set and hang and gives firmer pleats. It involves a fluid which may be a crease-resistant, crease-retaining or waterproofing agent. Don't ask for retexturing on knitted materials, woollens or lightweight fabrics.

Dry-cleaning is one of the best methods of moth-proofing but an extra treatment can be applied to give even more protection.

Articles which Need Special Treatment

Furnishings

Carpets, curtains, eiderdowns, duvets, pillows, cushions and loose covers should all be dealt with by a specialist cleaner.

Elaborate pelmets must be cleaned by hand and may have to be unpicked for cleaning.

Flame-retardant finishes will have to be re-applied each time the article is cleaned.

Leather and Suede

These require highly specialised cleaning, though local cleaners may be able to subcontract the cleaning to specialists.

Stain Removal

Suede and sheepskin should be cleaned as soon as any dirt begins to show round collar and cuffs. Very dirty garments may never become really clean again.

Leather and suede should be cleaned only in perchloroethylene.

Most cleaners will repair damaged cuffs, collars and pockets as an extra.

Some cleaners will touch up colours damaged during wear and many will match up buttons.

Pigskin

This is difficult to handle. If incorrect glues have been used, the lining will shrink. If the garment is cheap, the first cleaning may make the material harder, more wrinkled and generally less satisfactory.

Wool

There should be no water in the cleaning mixture for woollen garments. Most cleaners are well aware of this but mistakes have been known to happen so make sure your cleaner knows the garment is made of wool.

Treatment Before Taking a Garment to the Dry-Cleaner

- Always remove as much as you can of the spilled substance before it dries out. But don't attempt to remove the stain yourself unless past experience makes you absolutely sure you know how to do it.
- Don't rub, always dab.
- Don't use tissues for stain removal. A piece of clean white cotton is best.
- Home remedies can often make the problem worse. For instance, one supposed cure for red wine stains is to treat

them with white wine, but this leaves two stains instead of one and actually doubles the amount of work for the cleaner.

- If you spill something colourless that contains sugar (e.g. lemonade or fruit juice) or alcohol (e.g. white wine or perfume) take it to the dry-cleaner as quickly as possible. Stains of this kind may only become apparent after cleaning.
- Take dirty or stained garments to be cleaned as quickly as you can. The longer stains are left, the harder they will be to remove entirely.
- Draw the cleaner's attention to stains, explaining what the stain is and how long it has been there.
- Draw the cleaner's attention to any tears or loose hems or buttons, which can become worse during cleaning.
- If there is a belt with the garment to be cleaned, make sure this is noted on the ticket so you know there are two items to collect.
- Check pockets and linings for loose or sharp objects before leaving clothes at the dry-cleaner's.

Finding a Dry-Cleaner

- Ask locally. A shop's reputation spreads and you will soon find out which one offers the best service and prices.
- Look out for shops which belong to the Textile Services Association (TSA), the trade association for the textile services industry. Members display a blue and white window sticker with the current year's date on it. All Association members agree to observe a Code of Practice, drawn up in consultation with the Office of Fair Trading. It sets down requirements for the highest standards of service and provides a procedure for handling customer complaints, including a guarantee to pay fair compensation when loss or damage is the fault of the dry-cleaner.

Stain Removal

- The Dry-cleaning and Laundry Information Bureau (part of the TSA) can give details of a wide range of standard and specialist services offered by members of the TSA all over the country (see address on page 116).

Getting the Best From Your Dry-Cleaner

- Point out any stains that might need special treatment.
- Point out any tears which need repairing.
- Make sure the cleaner understands if an article is particularly old, valuable or delicate. He has the right to refuse to undertake to clean something if he feels it is too fragile or difficult.
- No reputable cleaner will actually guarantee to remove any kind of stain.
- Read the manufacturer's care instructions and if the label says 'Dry-Clean Only' don't try to wash it before taking it to the cleaner.
- Unless you are attempting to remove a simple stain on a robust fabric and you catch it at once, any stain is best left to the cleaner from the start.
- If there is no care label on the garment, try to tell the cleaner as much as you can about the fabric.
- Tea, coffee, fruit juices and curry are amongst the most difficult stains to remove, as they contain dyes which can be incorporated into the fibre of the cloth. Tell your cleaner if any of these has caused the stain.

Avoiding Problems

- Buy clothes and textiles from a reputable manufacturer.
- Be especially careful when buying brightly coloured pigskins, pale-coloured leathers, permanently pleated garments or richly coloured silks and fabrics with special effects (e.g. sequins, glitter and flocking).

- Read the care labels on garments carefully and follow the recommendations.
- Although care labelling has been adopted by most manufacturers, it is not compulsory. Try to buy articles with a care label securely attached.
- It is not sufficient for a garment to be labelled 'Dry-Clean Only'. The dry-cleaner will need to know which solvents he can safely use (denoted by 'A' or 'P' in a circle) and also the amount of heat the fabric will stand in the drying and pressing processes.
- Miracles cannot be performed on old articles.
- Curtains commonly cause problems, as exposure to sunlight can weaken their fabric to such an extent that they fall apart during dry-cleaning.

🐞 What to Do in Case of Complaint

- It is always best to make a formal complaint in writing to the manager or director of the cleaning company explaining your problem.
- Keep receipts and copies of all correspondence.
- If you receive no reply after ten days, or are not satisfied with the response, ask for help from your local Citizens Advice Bureau or Trading Standards Department of your local council.
- If the cleaner is a member of the TSA, contact them. They should be able to help sort out the problem (see page 117).
- If the cleaner is not a member, the TSA may still be able to advise you on what to do next.
- If the problem proves particularly difficult to resolve, the adviser may suggest an independent laboratory test on a 'loser pays' basis to see if the damage was caused by dry-cleaning. If the dry-cleaner is found to be at fault, under TSA rules you will receive fair compensation.

U_{seful} $A_{ddresses}$

 Advice

Citizens Advice Bureau

Look in the telephone directory for your local branch.

National Carpet Cleaners Association, 126 New Walk, De Montfort Street, Leicester LE1 7JA.
Will give names of local members.

Textile Services Association, 7 Churchill Court, 58 Station Road, North Harrow, Middlesex HA2 5SA.
Will give names of local and specialist members. Can help in case of complaint.

 Products

A. Bell & Co. Ltd., Kingsthorpe Works, Northampton.
Manufacturers of Bell's 1966 Cleaner; Bells 1967 Cleaner; Bell Marble Polish; Bell 'Touch-Up Pack'; Bell Marble Cleaner.

Dax Products Ltd., PO Box 119, Nottingham.
Manufacturers of Fungo fungicide (useful against mildew).

G. E. Holloway & Son (Engineering) Ltd., 12 Carlisle
Road, Colindale, London NW9 0HL.
Will give name of nearest stockist of Holloway's Chewing
Gum Remover and Rust Remover (good for rust on carpets
caused by leaking radiators).

Parker Pen Company, Service Department, PO Box 6,
Newhaven, Sussex BN9 0AX.
Will give stain removal instructions for all Parker Pen inks.

The Tarnprufe Company Ltd., 68 Nether Edge Road,
Sheffield S7 1RX.
Sells tarnish-inhibiting impregnated cloth bags for storing
silver.

Index

abrasives, 98
absorbents, 5, 98–9
acetate, 60
acetic acid, 17, 99
acetone, 108
acids, 17, 99–100
acrylic, 45, 60, 72, 73
adhesives, 19–20
alkalis, 20, 100–2
aluminium, 72–3
ammonia, 100
amyl acetate, 108
angora, 61
antiperspirants, 20

ballpoint pen, 21
bamboo, 76
baths, 73
beer, 21
beetroot, 21
bicarbonate of soda, 100
biological detergents, 7, 104
biological stains, 3
bird droppings, 21–2
blankets, 73–4
bleaches, 8, 102–4
blinds, 74
blood, 22
books, 74
borax, 101
brandy, 23
brass, 74–5
bricks, 75
brocade, 61
bronze, 75
burns, 93
butter, 23

camel hair, 61
candle wax, 23
cane, 76
canvas blinds, 74
car polish, 23–4
caramel, 24
carbon paper, 24
carpets, 3, 106, 111

cashmere, 61
cast iron pans, 85
castor oil and zinc ointment, 59
caustic soda, 20
cavalry twill, 61
chenille, 62
chewing gum, 24–5
chiffon, 62
china, 76
chintz, 62
chlorine bleach, 102
chocolate, 25
chrome, 76
cigarette burns, 93
citric acid, 99
cleaning agents, 98–109
Coca Cola, 26
cocoa, 25
cod liver oil, 26
coffee, 27
colour-fastness, 9
colour removers, 102
concrete floors, 76
contact adhesive, 19
cooking pans, 73, 77
copper, 77
corduroy, 62
cork, 77
cotton, 62
crayons, 27
cream, 27–8
cretonne, 63
crude oil, 28
curry, 28
cyanoacrylates, 19

dab and blot technique, 12–13
damask, 63
decanters, 77–8
denim, 63
detergents, 5–7, 104
diluting cleaning agents, 50
disinfectants, 105
dried stains, 4–5
dry-cleaning, 7–8, 108–9, 110–15